VIENNA

SURVIVAL GUIDE

FOR EDUCATION

Vienna Survival Guide for Education
Copyright © 2019
HOME TOWN MEDIA GMBH

ISBN 978-3-200-06532-1
Printed and bound by Ferdinand Berger & Söhne GmbH

CONTENT AND PRODUCTION
Home Town Media GmbH
Praterstraße 1, Space 21
1020 Vienna, Austria

PUBLISHER Margaret Childs

EDITORIAL MANAGEMENT Alyssa-Ninja Weis

WRITERS Michael Bernstein,
Magdalena Schwarz

COPY EDITOR Anthony Mills

PROOFREADING Pary Smith

PROOFREADING Mahnoor Jalal

GRAPHIC DESIGN AND ILLUSTRATIONS Karin Dreher, karin-grafikdesign.com

PRINTING AND BINDING
Ferdinand Berger & Söhne GmbH
Wiener Straße 80
A-3580 Horn

CONTENTS

COLOR KEY

GETTING
STARTED

CHILDREN'S
EDUCATION

TEENAGE
EDUCATION

ADULT
EDUCATION

DIRECTORY

GLOSSARY

GETTING STARTED

Preview:
what this book does and doesn't cover

The SURVIVAL GUIDE FOR EDUCATION is a guide for parents of school-age children, for university students and for fans of life-long learning. Do note that while much of the information is equally applicable to other provinces, the focus of this guide is on the Austrian capital.

Providing a comprehensive overview of the Austrian education system, this guide zooms in on the questions that concern non-Austrians staying long-term or short-term in Vienna. Throughout the book, testimonials shed light on the challenges faced and the solutions found by your fellow expats. On the final pages (see p 265-275), there's also an extensive glossary of the German technical terms you're bound to encounter at the playground, at parent-teacher conferences or in all those forms you will inevitably have to fill out.

TERMINOLOGY
used in this guide

Parent/legal guardian

Please keep in mind that when we use the term "parent" in this guide, we also mean legal guardians and other primary caretakers.

Student/pupil

In Austria, the word *Student* is reserved for students at a university or a university of applied sciences (*Fachhochschule*). To preclude misunderstandings, we use "pupil" exclusively to refer to children and teenagers through secondary school, and "student" to refer to those attending tertiary education.

Pre-school, primary, secondary, tertiary and adult education

The Austrian school system is complicated, and the confusing terminology doesn't help. For instance, we start counting from the beginning again after primary school, which means what is actually the fifth year of schooling (i.e., the first year at an AHS or NMS) is called first grade (*Erste Klasse*). As this is likely unclear to most non-Austrian readers, we have decided to use the terms primary, secondary, tertiary, and adult education in this guide. Here are the age spans these grades typically refer to:

* Pre-school: ages 0 to 6
* Primary school: four years, ages 6 to 9/10
* Secondary school: divided into lower secondary (4 years, ages 10/11 to 14) and upper secondary (4 years, ages 15 to 18/19)
* Tertiary school: university and other tertiary education institutions (ages 18/19 and above)
* Adult education and second-chance education: anything beyond compulsory and tertiary education

At least nine years of schooling are compulsory in Austria (see Secondary School, p 122).

RESOURCES
beyond this guide

Throughout the book, and especially at the end (see Directory, p 259), we point out additional sources of information, counseling and advice.

Parents of school-age children, for example, should seize the opportunities offered to visit schools. You can do this on the Day of Viennese Schools (*Tag der Wiener Schulen*) in early to mid-October, on which 670 Viennese schools open their doors to interested visitors. Parents and their children are also advised to attend "open house" days (*Tag der offenen Tür*) held by most schools. You can find the open-house dates for all Viennese schools here:

 wien.gv.at

Another opportunity to get a feel for a school is *Schnuppern*, which means that after a pre-registration, your child can spend a regular school day at a school of your choice, usually free of charge – just contact the school you're interested in.

You can find information on free support and counseling services related to administrative, legal and psychological matters on the last pages of this guide (see Directory, p 259). For example, the website of the City of Vienna (**wien.gv.at/english/education-research**) and this visualization (**bildungssystem.at/en**) of the Austrian education system may be helpful. Another great online resource is provided by the public employment service Austria (**ausbildungskompass.at/en**). Last but not least, the expat center, a part of the Vienna business agency, offers individual counseling in 17 languages.

INTRO-DUCTION

From *Hofrat* to MSc: a brief history of schooling in Austria

MARIA THERESIA AND THE BEGINNING OF COMPULSORY SCHOOLING

Compulsory education has a long tradition in Austria. In 1774, Empress Maria Theresia introduced six years of compulsory schooling. In 1869, eight years of education became mandatory, and today, obligatory schooling ends after nine years. The first educational reforms have been followed by countless more, and in today's politics, education spurs passionate debates in parliament. Conservatives and liberals have divergent philosophies, and as a result, the Austrian education system is in a constant state of flux. Ratification of the most recent reform package, the 2018 Pedagogics Package (*Pädagogikpaket*), started only recently (see Continuous Politics and Reforms, p 18) At the time of publication it is not possible to foresee which parts, if any, of the package will be confirmed by a government emerging from the general election in September 2019.

This SURVIVAL GUIDE FOR EDUCATION will tell you everything you need to know about the Austrian education system, focusing on the questions you and other non-Austrians have likely asked yourselves, such as: Should my bilingual child go to an international or to a regular Austrian school? Which options do kids have after compulsory education? Can I study at the university for free even if I don't have Austrian citizenship? Where can I learn Chinese or acquire skills in business administration as an adult?

But first, let's look at an Austrian trait almost as uniquely *österreichisch* as Mozart and *Wiener Schnitzel:* the obsession with titles (*Titelwahn*)!

THE AUSTRIAN LOVE OF TITLES

Whether in the doctor's office, at business meetings or in a traditional Viennese *Kaffeehaus*, you will likely have observed that Austrians are obsessed with academic titles. In this country, around 1,500 academic and job titles are regulated by law, making Austria one of the love-of-title front-runners relative to the size of its population. The reasons why titles like *Magister* and *Diplom-Ingenieurin* are so dear to the national soul are historical. The Habsburg monarchy was so vast that title-based hierarchies were a necessity, especially in the military administration. The monarchs also realized that handing out fancy ranks fostered motivation just as much as pay raises – without straining the imperial treasuries. Today, thanks to the Bologna reforms (see The Bologna Process, p 192) and an increasing internationalization in business and academia, the title obsession has started subsiding. For example, while in the past the Burgtheater online subscription form would make you scroll through 200 title options, now titles have been reduced to a total of nine. Nevertheless, when applying for a job in Austria, you are well advised to include your academic titles next to your name on your CV. You never know, that MSc or MBA might still give you a head start.

The EDUCATION SYSTEM in facts & figures

CONTINUOUS POLITICS AND REFORMS

Education is the subject of constant and heated debate in Austria, so it's no surprise that each new government proclaims major reform ideas. The most recent education reform, the Pedagogics Package (*Pädagogikpaket*), was presented in 2018 and is partly ratified. The three main changes so far are the re-introduction of number grades (*Ziffernnoten* from 1 for very good to 5 for insufficient) on top of verbal assessments in primary schools, the possibility of achievement-based student groupings in the *Neue Mittelschule* (see NMS: New Secondary School, p X), and the addition of a voluntary 10th year of schooling at pre-vocational schools (*Polytechnische Schulen*) (see Pre-Vocational School and Dual Vocational Education and Training, p X). To stay up to date with ongoing changes to school law, check out the Ministry of Education's website:

bildung.bmbwf.gv.at (only partly in English).

PISA RANKINGS

While many Austrian public schools offer high-quality education for little to no money, there is certainly room for improvement. The Program for International Student Assessment (PISA) is an international study conducted by the Organization for Economic Co-operation and Development (OECD), which evaluates and compares the educational systems in around 90 participating countries. Every three years, 15-year-old pupils attending public or private schools take part in standardized tests in mathematics, science and reading. Unfortunately, Austria's most recent PISA results from 2015 were less than impressive, considering that it is still one of the richest nations in the world. Austrian pupils are around average in most areas, and trail behind the OECD average in reading skills. In contrast to many other countries, there are also significant gender differences: Girls are better readers, while boys are ahead in math and science. On top, Austria's education system appears to favor pupils without migration background and pupils whose parents hold academic degrees. In 2015, children of academics achieved around 100 points more, on average, than pupils whose parents completed lower secondary school, which implies a lead of about two years of learning.

MEAN PISA SCORES (2015)
OF 10 SELECTED COUNTRIES

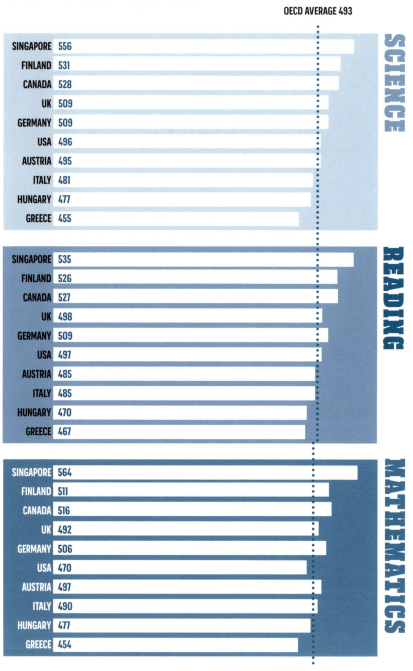

OECD AVERAGE 493

SCIENCE

SINGAPORE	556
FINLAND	531
CANADA	528
UK	509
GERMANY	509
USA	496
AUSTRIA	495
ITALY	481
HUNGARY	477
GREECE	455

READING

SINGAPORE	535
FINLAND	526
CANADA	527
UK	498
GERMANY	509
USA	497
AUSTRIA	485
ITALY	485
HUNGARY	470
GREECE	467

MATHEMATICS

SINGAPORE	564
FINLAND	511
CANADA	516
UK	492
GERMANY	506
USA	470
AUSTRIA	497
ITALY	490
HUNGARY	477
GREECE	454

Source: OECD 2015

OECD AVERAGE 490

PARENTS' SOCIOECONOMIC STATUS AND OTHER PREDICTORS OF SCHOOL SUCCESS

National statistics also reflect the patterns of the PISA results. In comparison to other European countries, Austria spends a slightly higher proportion of its gross domestic product on education and research. So far, these efforts have not led to the elimination of substantial inequalities. After primary school, pupils transfer either to the academically-oriented *AHS* system (see AHS: Academic Secondary School, p 125), typically leading to the *Matura* (the Austrian higher-education entrance examination) and an academic degree, or to the vocationally-oriented *NMS* system (see NMS: New Secondary School, p 133), after which many move on to vocational schools. Problematically, a full 71% of prospective *AHS* pupils have a parent who has at least the *Matura*, while this is the case for only a third of prospective *NMS* students. In Vienna, 42.7% of people have a non-Austrian background, and this again appears to impact school choice: Children with German as a first language transfer to the *AHS* more frequently than children with a non-German mother tongue.

Education in Austria: THE BASICS

The Austrian education system in a nutshell? All children from age 6 to 15 who live in Austria must go to school, and this also applies to children of asylum-seekers and refugees. State-run schools are free of charge, while private schools and private schools under public law charge monthly tuition fees ranging from around €150 to €600 or higher.

Private schools under public law *(Privatschulen mit Öffentlichkeitsrecht)* are essentially private schools that are officially accredited (see Public and Private Schools, p 24).

If you are the parent of a child of compulsory school age, you should receive an invitation letter from the city education authority in Vienna (or your provincial education authority if you live in a different part of Austria). You and your child may then participate in the personal registration process at your local school. If you don't speak German well enough, consider bringing an interpreter if you can (see Admission to Secondary School, p 158).

Public schools accept children who speak very little German as so-called non-regular pupils (*außerordentliche/r Schüler/in*). This means that while they attend school with the other children and can also advance to the respective next level, they are granted two years in which they are not graded and can acquire basic German language skills. Schools also usually offer language-support courses.

In public schools, all pupils receive free school books for all subjects, and bilingual children can request books on German as a second language as well as bilingual dictionaries.

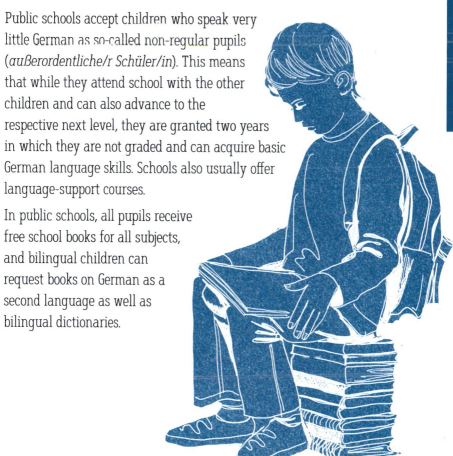

PUBLIC AND PRIVATE SCHOOLS

Around half of the primary schools in Vienna are private, according to the City of Vienna. Note that in Austria many private schools are, in fact, so-called private schools under public law (*Private Pflichtschulen mit Öffentlichkeitsrecht*), which means that the school reports they award are officially accredited and thus legally on par with school reports from public schools.

Private schools under public law are also required to largely follow the same curriculum (*Lehrplan*) as public schools. By contrast, private schools not under public law (*Private Pflichtschulen ohne Öffentlichkeitsrecht*) are not officially accredited, and their pupils must take yearly external exams (see Higher Education Entrance Examination for External Students, p 249).

In Austria, 6% of primary school pupils and 9.9% of secondary school pupils (NMS & AHS) are in private schools; in Vienna the percentages are 16.2% and 16.3%, respectively, and these numbers are currently increasing. But are Austrian private schools better than their public counterparts? While this is a hard question to answer, international studies tend to show that pupils with similar socioeconomic backgrounds perform equally well, whether they attend private or public schools. The 2015 PISA results (see p 20) on the science performance of Austrian pupils even showed that, after accounting for the influence of socioeconomic profiles, pupils in public schools, on average, scored higher than those in private schools. Still, private schools have more funds for additional activities and afternoon care, and, most decisively, they get to choose their pupils. Public schools are required to favor children living nearby, while private schools can pick pupils based on their own selection criteria. Monthly tuition fees in private schools are between €150 and €200 and €400 and €600 including lunches and afternoon care (international schools are an exception).

Ultimately, it is probably best to research, visit schools and pick the one that suits you – whether public or private. You will learn the differences betweenand details about Vienna's public and private schools, including international and bilingual ones, in the following sections.

HOMESCHOOLING

Homeschooling has never been as big in Austria as in other countries, although it is legally possible. Generally speaking, you can meet the official standards of compulsory schooling by teaching your kids yourself at home or having them attend a private school not accredited under public law *(Privatschulen ohne Öffentlichkeitsrecht)*. Parents simply need to apply for homeschooling at the beginning of each school year and make sure the education their children receive is at least equivalent to that offered at public schools. At the end of each year, the pupils need to undergo an external exam *(Externistenprüfung)*. In 2017/2018, a total of 2,320 children were being homeschooled in Austria, a number that is increasing but overall still negligible. On the whole, Austrians view the concept of homeschooling with a healthy dose of skepticism, so parents determined to homeschool should prepare for raised eyebrows. Since the public and accredited private education sector offers a range of options, from religious schools and schools with musical, artistic or sport focuses, to schools with alternative pedagogic concepts, parents are likely to find a good fit for their child beyond homeschooling.

GRADING FROM 1 TO 5

Scholastic achievements are usually graded with scores from 1 to 5. A grade of 1 for "very good" (*Sehr gut*) is the best grade, followed by 2 for "good" (*Gut*), 3 for "satisfactory" (*Befriedigend*), 4 for "sufficient" (*Genügend*), and 5 for "insufficient" (*Nicht genügend*). Grades 1 to 4 are all passing grades, and 5 is the only fail grade. According to school laws, only academic achievements beyond what is to be expected deserve a *Sehr gut*. In primary schools, integrative schools (*Sonderschulen*, special needs schools) and NMSs, the class forum (*Klassenforum*, which includes the teacher plus parents) or school forum (*Schulforum*, which includes the headteacher, all teachers and parents operating as spokespeople for each class) can decide that pupils should receive verbal reports in addition to numerical grades. In most schools, pupils receive a preliminary written report (*Semesterzeugnis*) at the end of the winter term in February, and a final written report (*Jahreszeugnis*) at the end of the summer term in June.

While the majority of Viennese schools use the 1-5 grading system, there are exceptions: the American International School uses the US grading scale, the Lycée Français uses the French system, and most international schools use the IB (International Baccalaureate) system. Find an approximate comparison of grading scales below.

COMPARISON OF INTERNATIONAL GRADING SCALES

	PASS												FAIL	
Austria	**1** (Sehr gut)			**2** (Gut)			**3** (Befriedigend)			**4** (Genügend)			**5** (Nicht genügend)	
US	A+ (100-97) GPA: 4.3	A (96.9-93) GPA: 4.0	A- (92.9-90) GPA: 3.7	B+ (89.9-87) GPA: 3.3	B (86.9-83) GPA: 3.0	B- (82.9-80) GPA: 2.7	C+ (79.9-77) GPA: 2.3	C (76.9-73) GPA: 2.0	C- (72.9-70) GPA: 1.7	D+ (69.9-67) GPA: 1.3	D (66.9-63) GPA: 1.0	D- (62.9-60)	F (59.9-0) GPA: 0.0	
France	**Très honorable** avec félicitations du jury (20-18)	**Très bien** (17.99-16)		**Bien** (15.99-14)			**Assez bien** (13.99-12)			**Passable** (11.99-10)			**Échec** (9.99-0)	
IB*	**7** (Excellent)	**6** (Very good)		**5** (Good)			**4** (Satisfactory)			**3** (Mediocre)			**2** (Poor)	**1** (Very poor)

* International Baccalaureate

Sources: Princeton University of German, Wikipedia

SCHOOL YEAR AND HOLIDAYS

The school year is usually divided into two terms, with the winter term lasting from September to February, and the summer term from February to June. While exact dates differ from year to year and between provinces, the general school holidays include: one week between the two terms in February *(Semesterferien);* one-and-a-half weeks for Easter *(Osterferien);* four days around Pentecost *(Pfingstferien),* nine weeks in the summer *(Sommerferien);* five days in October *(Herbstferien);* and two weeks around Christmas *(Weihnachtsferien).*

In addition, and to the frustration of parents scrambling to organize babysitters, there are five extra days off per year (*schulautonome freie Tage),* at least three of them chosen by the school and the rest determined by Vienna's Department of Education (*Bildungsdirektion für Wien*). Often, these extra days are scheduled as bridging days (*Fenstertage*) through proximity to a weekend or a holiday, to create a mini-vacation.

OF COURSE, SCHOOLS ARE ALSO CLOSED ON THE COUNTLESS AUSTRIAN CATHOLIC AND CIVIC HOLIDAYS, WHICH YOU CAN LOOK UP HERE:

feiertage-oesterreich.at In addition, members of a few other religious communities (e.g. Protestant, Jewish) are allowed to stay home from school on certain religious holidays.

Beware, some international schools keep their gates closed on specific days (the American International School, for instance, gives pupils a day off on American Thanksgiving). Schools will typically inform students about holiday dates, but you can check out the differences between provinces here:

schulferien.org

BIG DECISIONS:
THE NMS/AHS DIVIDE

Many parents are worried about a parting of ways at the end of primary school, when their children are around 10 years old. That's when Austrian pupils transfer either to an AHS or to an NMS. Some parents believe this one decision will determine their children's future, and it is true that the AHS track traditionally leads toward the *Matura* and tertiary studies, while pupils on the NMS track often go on to complete apprenticeships and other types of vocational training. However, the Austrian education system, with its many different school types and educational pathways, is permeable. Pupils who perform well at an NMS often transfer to higher vocational education schools leading to the *Reife-* and *Diplomprüfung*, which is equivalent to the *Matura* (see Secondary School, p 128). In addition, there are several opportunities to catch up on qualifications and pass a higher education entrance exam later on in life (see Second Chance Education, p 247).

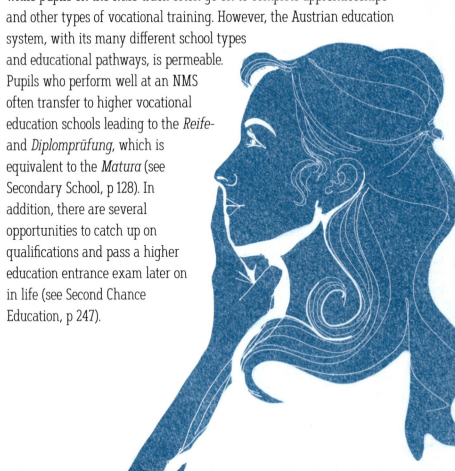

TESTIMONIALS

DANIEL, 27

teacher and coordinator, Amadeus International School Vienna

I work at Amadeus International School Vienna, which is a day and boarding school with an integrated Music and Arts Academy. Our school is also an International Baccalaureate (IB) Continuum School, which means that the school follows the IB curriculum and that pupils can opt to sit the IB diploma. In my experience, two reasons why parents and students choose our school are the music academy and the fact that we offer boarding, which is attractive for students from overseas. In addition, the school emphasizes „service learning," which means that students are encouraged to come up with community service projects, such as visiting senior homes, donating games to orphanages, or organizing sports tournaments for charitable causes. After graduation, the majority of our pupils go on to study at tertiary education institutions abroad. Personally, I think that each and every school has its own identity, culture, and advantages and disadvantages. I recommend visiting different schools and going to open house days or booking school tours, so that parents can make the right decision for their child.

MATTHEW, 37,

self-employed language trainer

I was born in Sydney, Australia, and moved to Austria in 2005. In Australia, the education system is fairly standardized. Everybody goes to one high school and the school hours stay basically the same from primary school until the end of high school. There is relatively little corruption or bureaucracy and transparency is a priority. This would be a large culture shock for me in Austria. When my children began their education, I was confronted with the maze that is schooling in Austria. I must admit I am still not completely sure how it all works but am armed with the knowledge from friends that all that really matters is the quality of the teacher in the classroom. I was shocked that people look at the percentage of migrants in schools here and generally avoid those with high numbers. In Australia, due to our strict immigration system, a school with many children from non-English-speaking backgrounds will usually be one of the best schools in the country. As always in Vienna, it is about contacts, contacts, contacts. A school may create a new website or a new government bureaucracy may be created to provide information, but word of mouth still rules and the numerous rules seem to be always flexible. I am quite encouraged by the growth of new private schools that seem to offer flexibility and new methods of teaching children.

VERONICA, 40

good governance expert/ international consultant

My family and I relocated to Vienna from Moldova in 2018. My oldest daughter, who was then 18, had spent grade 11 at an American high school and loved it. She couldn't really imagine going back to her Moldovan high school, so we ended up looking for a high school with a focus on music and singing in Vienna. Our daughter did several interviews and admissions tests, and we finally decided on a Waldorf school, the Rudolf Steiner Landschule in Schönau, Lower Austria. This school seemed to check all the boxes: Situated in a former castle in a small forest, it gave off a familiar feel, and our daughter could benefit from its art and music focus in grade 12. We also enrolled our other two daughters, age 3 and 13, and paid a total monthly tuition fee of €800-€870. You usually get a discount the more kids you register.

Although we were initially happy with our choice, the school did not provide any German-language support, and our daughters also longed for a more academically stringent environment. Luckily, our oldest daughter, after going to several open days and mastering an audition, was accepted into an amazing program on singing and songwriting at the Vienna Music Institute.

Our second-oldest daughter transferred to a public computer science *Mittelschule*, the Neue Niederösterreichische Informatikmitellschule Leobersdorf. I became aware of some of the prejudice people have regarding the NMS, but I have to emphasize that, based on our experience, these stereotypes are unfounded. The school has an innovative pedagogical approach, and the infrastructure, the quality of the education and the support from teachers were brilliant. Our daughter got weekly German tutoring, and her grades are so good that she now, after she completes school in 2020, wants to continue in an international school or in a *Gymnasium* in Vienna.

Our youngest daughter attends the local music school and community-organized German classes, and she'll start kindergarten in the fall. All in all, I am very impressed with the Austrian public education system.

SYSTEM

	PRE-SCHOOL	PRIMARY EDUCATION	LOWER SECONDARY EDUCATION
Typical age	0 to 6	6 to 9/10	10/11 to 14
School years		1 to 4	5 to 8
	COMPULSORY EDUCATION		
Available school type	Public (*Städtische*) kindergartens (see p 67)	Public primary school (*Volksschule*) (see p 98)	AHS (lower secondary) (see p 126)
	Private kindergartens (see p 71, 83)	Experimental (*Schulversuche*, see p 99)	
	Small-group day care (*Tageseltern*) (see p 72)	Private / denominational primary school (see p 100)	NMS (see p 133)
	Children's groups self-governed by parents (*Kindergruppen*) (see p 73)		
	International / English-language private kindergartens (see p 70)	Bilingual progams (see p 46)	Bilingual programs (see p 46)
		Private international schools (see p 53)	Private international schools (see p 33)
	Home care (see p 75)	Home schooling / alternative schools (p 142)	
	Integrative/special needs (see p 76)	Integrative/special needs (see p 76)	Integrative/special needs NMS (see p 134)

SOURCE: BILDUNGSSYSTEM.AT

Visual overview of the Austrian education system

COMPLETION OF COMPULSORY SCHOOLING	HIGHER SECONDARY EDUCATION	ENTRANCE TO TERTIARY EDUCATION	TERTIARY EDUCATION	ADULT AND SECOND-CHANCE EDUCATION
15/16	15-18/19	-	18/19 and above	18/19 and above
9	9 to 12/13			
AHS (higher secondary) (see p 130)		*Matura* (see p 146)	University (see p 200) University of applied sciences (see p 211)	Adult education (see p 251) Second-chance education (see p 247)
School for higher vocational education (BHS, see p 140)		Diplom- und Reifeprüfung (see p 146)		
Lehre mit Matura (see p 136)		Berufsreifeprüfung (see p 152)	University college of teacher education (see p 214)	
Dual vocational training, etc. (see p 139)		Studienberechti-gungsprüfung (see p 250)	Colleges (see p 141)	
School for intermediate vocational education (BMS, see p 140)				
Bilingual programs (see p 46)		*Matura* / IB (see p 128)		
Private international schools (see p 53)				
		Externistenprüfung (see p 150)		
Integrative vocational training (see p 134)				

A MYRIAD OF
TRAJECTORIES!

The visualization on the previous page clearly shows why the Austrian education system can be so puzzling to non-Austrians!

First of all, you can choose between several school types at each educational level (pre-school, primary, secondary, tertiary, post-tertiary, adult and second-chance education). Very broadly speaking, there are public versus private schools, monolingual versus bilingual/international schools, and more academically-oriented versus more vocationally-oriented schools. As if this were not complicated enough, there are also schools that fall between these binary categories: for instance, the *BHS* (see school for higher vocational education, p 140) combines an academic education with vocational training.

FOR THE SAKE OF CLARITY,

the visualization on page 34-35 focuses on the principal Austrian types of schools, and it reflects the most typical pathways of education. Still, the Austrian system often enables pupils to switch between the default tracks, as long as their academic performance allows it. For example, a pupil who has completed the lower secondary AHS, and who plans on later studying architecture, engineering or design at university, might be well-advised to transfer to an HTL (see school for higher vocational education, p 140), where he or she can pass the *Reifeprüfung* and *Diplomprüfung* (see p 146) and at the same time acquire relevant technical abilities, such as structural design or project management.

WHICH SCHOOL IS THE RIGHT ONE FOR YOUR CHILD?

YOUR CHILD IS...

... younger than 5/6 years old ...

... and you're looking for child care or a pre-school:

- Public (*Städtische*) kindergartens (p 67)
- International/English-language private kindergartens (p 70)
- German-language private kindergartens (p 71)
- Small-group day care (*Tageseltern*) (p 72)
- Children's groups self-governed by parents (*Kindergruppen*) (p 73)
- After-school day care (*Hort*) (p 74)
- Home care (p 75)
- Integrative (special needs) care (p 76)

... between 6 and 10 years old ...

... and you prefer German-language instruction

- Public primary school (plus optional German language classes) (p 98)
- Experimental primary school (*Schulversuche*) (p 99)
- Private/denominational primary school (p 100)
- Homeschooling/alternative schools (p 142)

... and your child has native English proficiency and you do not feel they need to acquire German at native-speaker level

- Private international schools (p 53)

... and you prefer bilingual instruction, so that your child learns German

- Bilingual programs (p 46)

The decision tree below will help you choose the educational options that are best for your family, and it tells you where to find relevant information in this guide. (Note that this graphic is a simplification of the Austrian education system and shows only the most typical educational pathways).

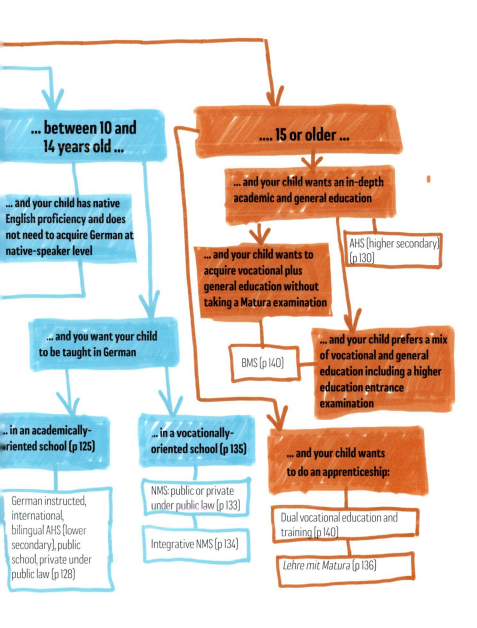

... between 10 and 14 years old ...

... and your child has native English proficiency and does not need to acquire German at native-speaker level

.... 15 or older ...

... and your child wants an in-depth academic and general education

AHS (higher secondary) (p 130)

... and your child wants to acquire vocational plus general education without taking a Matura examination

... and you want your child to be taught in German

BMS (p 140)

... and your child prefers a mix of vocational and general education including a higher education entrance examination

.. in an academically-oriented school (p 125)

... in a vocationally-oriented school (p 135)

... and your child wants to do an apprenticeship:

German instructed, international, bilingual AHS (lower secondary), public school, private under public law (p 128)

NMS: public or private under public law (p 133)

Integrative NMS (p 134)

Dual vocational education and training (p 140)

Lehre mit Matura (p 136)

WHICH EDUCATIONAL OPTION IS RIGHT FOR YOU?

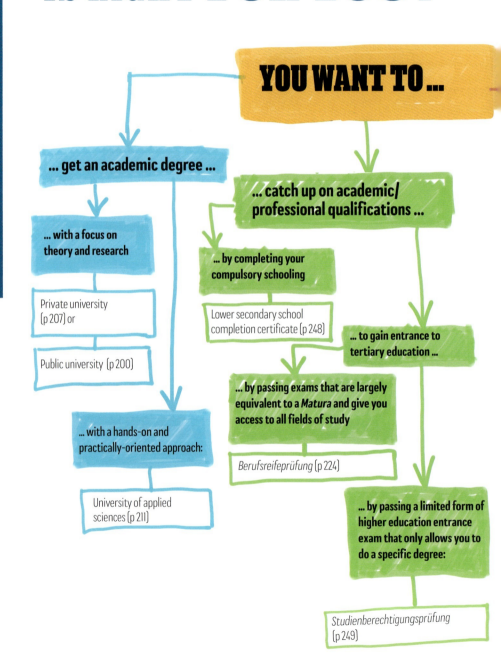

YOU WANT TO ...

... get an academic degree ...

... with a focus on theory and research

Private university (p 207) or

Public university (p 200)

... with a hands-on and practically-oriented approach:

University of applied sciences (p 211)

... catch up on academic/ professional qualifications ...

... by completing your compulsory schooling

Lower secondary school completion certificate (p 248)

... to gain entrance to tertiary education ...

... by passing exams that are largely equivalent to a *Matura* and give you access to all fields of study

Berufsreifeprüfung (p 224)

... by passing a limited form of higher education entrance exam that only allows you to do a specific degree:

Studienberechtigungsprüfung (p 249)

This decision tree leads you to the educational opportunity that best fits your wishes, and it tells you where to find the relevant information in this guide. (This visualization is a simplification of the Austrian education system and shows only the most typical educational pathways).

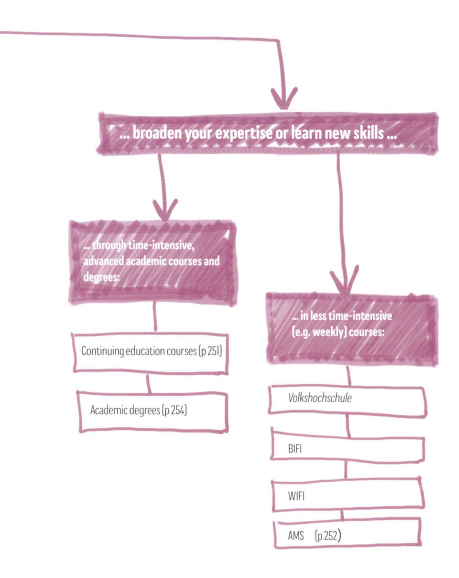

... broaden your expertise or learn new skills ...

... through time-intensive, advanced academic courses and degrees:

... in less time-intensive (e.g. weekly) courses:

Continuing education courses (p 251)

Academic degrees (p 254)

Volkshochschule

BIFI

WIFI

AMS   (p 252)

BILINGUAL & ENGLISH-LANGUAGE SCHOOLING

Whether you and your children are planning to stay in Vienna for only a few months or a number of years, **learning German will enhance your quality of life here** and provide a valuable, lifelong advantage, particularly for children.

Fortunately, Vienna affords many educational opportunities for pupils and students whose mother tongue is not German – from international schools to bilingual programs and rapid immersive German instruction.

In the 2016/17 school year, over **115,000 pupils** **(58,000 of them foreign)** whose mother tongue was not German attended Vienna's schools.

Public schools
FOR PUPILS WITHOUT
NATIVE-GERMAN ABILITY

For all pupils whose German ability is not up to par (designated, unfortunately, as "non-regular pupils"), special assistance support is available as early as the pre-school level.

If a primary school pupil has little or no German knowledge, he or she will be placed in an age-appropriate class, but will not be graded. Results from a standardized test will help the Board of Education decide if a pupil should be placed in a special German class or German course, provided cost-free for a maximum of four semesters.

With German classes (*Deutschförderklassen*), primary school pupils receive 15 hours and secondary school pupils receive 20 hours per week of intensive German lessons *as part of* their total weekly instruction. With German courses (*Deutschförderkurse*), six hours of German lessons are given *parallel to* normal weekly instruction.

If necessary, after two years, further measures are possible.

Bilingual programs

Most secondary schools offer English as the primary living-language subject. Two public schools offer French, and one Russian, as well. While all public schools integrate foreign-language instruction into their standard curricula, some special schools offer varying levels of bilingual instruction in multiple subjects. Using the pedagogic concept of Content and Language Integrated Learning (CLIL), these schools pair native language teachers (non-German) with local teachers in the classroom.

VIENNA BILINGUAL SCHOOLING (VBS)

Offered at a few public primary and secondary schools, VBS is an experimental school program for pupils with outstanding command (mother-tongue or second language) of both English and German. Most courses are taught in both langua-ges by local and native speakers. VBS classes strive to admit equal numbers of German and English native-speaker pupils.

Admission to VBS is more selective than a stan-dard school (see criteria in the following sections) and requires an orientation interview and in some cases a special test (Aufnahmeprüfung). Demand is high and available places are limited. Siblings of students already enrolled are given admissions preference. Pupils who have attended a VBS primary school are more likely to be admitted to a VBS secondary school.

VBS PRIMARY SCHOOLS:

* Astrid-Lindgren-Schule, Sonnenuhrgasse 3, 1060 Vienna
* VBS Keplerplatz, Keplerplatz 7, 1100 Vienna
* Marie Jahoda Schule, Herbststraße 86, 1160 Vienna
* VBS Scheibenbergstraße, Scheibenbergstraße 63, 1180 Vienna
* VBS Grinzinger Straße, Grinzinger Straße 88, 1190 Vienna
* VBS Kaisermühlen, Schüttaustraße 42, 1220 Vienna
* VBS Donaucity, Leonard-Bernstein-Straße 2, 1220 Vienna
* VBS/GEPS Meißnergasse, Meißnergasse 1, 1220 Vienna

VBS SECONDARY SCHOOLS:

* Realgymnasium/WRG 8 Feldgasse, Feldgasse 6-8, 1080 Vienna
* NMS Wendstattgasse,* Wendstattgasse 3, 1100 Vienna
* Realgymnasium 14 Linzer Straße, Linzer Straße 146, 1140 Vienna
* NMS Koppstraße,* Koppstraße 110/II, 1160 Vienna
* Gymnasium Parhamerplatz, Parhamerplatz 18, 1170 Vienna
* NMS In der Krim,* In der Krim 6, 1190 Vienna
* Realgymnasium Krottenbachstraße, Krottenbachstraße 11, 1190 Vienna
* Gymnasium/Realgymnasium 22, Theodor-Kramer-Straße 3, 1220 Vienna
* Gymnasium Draschestraße, Draschestraße 90-92, 1230 Vienna

(* NMS = New Secondary School, 5th – 8th
school years only).

OTHER BILINGUAL PROGRAMS

While only a handful of schools offer VBS, several others emphasize bilingual teaching in the classroom (also using English native speakers to support local teachers); however, most instruction is still carried out in German.

DUAL-LANGUAGE PROGRAM (DLP)

In primary and secondary schools offering DLP, pupils are taught according to standard public school lesson plans, but with a few extra weekly hours of English instruction and additional support from native-speaker teachers in subjects such as math, geography and biology. Admissions preference is given to pupils who have received previous bilingual instruction, who are themselves English native speakers or who show above-average talent in English.

 **Listing of DLP schools:
schulentwicklung.at**

GLOBAL EDUCATION PRIMARY SCHOOL (GEPS)

These primary schools combine intensive English instruction with "global education" as an integral part of the curriculum; they employ English native-speaker teachers and make stronger use of Information and Communication Technologies (ICT).

EUROPEAN PRIMARY SCHOOL (EPS)

Currently offered in only two primary schools in Vienna, the EPS system is similar to the GEPS one but is woven into European education projects, in particular with neighboring countries Czech Republic, Hungary and Slovakia. Starting in the third school year, additional foreign language courses are taught.

* Neustiftgasse 98 – 102, 1070 Vienna
* Goldschlagstraße 14-16, 1150 Vienna

EUROPEAN MIDDLE SCHOOL /
EUROPEAN HIGH SCHOOL (EMS / EHS)

English instruction in these schools is focused on European studies. Other modern languages, including Slavic languages of neighboring countries, are offered as well.

* EMS Neustiftgasse, Neustiftgasse 98-102, 1070 Vienna
* EHS Henriettenplatz 6, 1150 Vienna

JUNIOR HIGH SCHOOL (JHS), LOWER-LEVEL ONLY

A few experimental New Secondary Schools (NMS) use English native-speaker team teaching and focus on the English language as used in the workplace.

* JHS Carlbergergasse 72, 1230 Vienna has a focus on social studies, arts and science.
* JHS Konsstanziagasse 50, 1220 Vienna has a focus on information technology and science.

NON-ENGLISH BILINGUAL INSTRUCTION

Some public schools offer bilingual instruction in other languages, using native-speaker team teachers.

FRENCH:

* Primary school: FIP - Français intégré à l'école primaire – is offered at Volkschule Stubenbastei 3, 1010 Vienna. Less intensive Papillon classes are offered at Volkschule Köhlergasse 9, 1180 Vienna.

* Secondary school: FIPS - Français intégré dans les projets au secondaire – is offered at the Akademisches Gymnasium Beethovenplatz 1, 1010 Vienna.

ITALIAN:

* Primary school: SIB - Scuola Elementare Italiana Bilingue – is offered at Volkschule Europa Schule, Vorgartengasse 95-97, 1200 Vienna.

SPANISH:

* Primary school: Arco Iris is offered at Marie Jahoda Schule, Herbststraße 86, 1160 Vienna. Less intensive Mariposa classes are offered at: VS Kolonitzgasse 15, 1030 Vienna; VS Reichsapfelgasse 30, 1150 Vienna; and Integrative Schule Hernals, Hernalser Hauptstraße 220, 1170 Vienna.

* Secondary school (lower-level):SIM – Spanisch in der Mittelschule – is offered at NMS Kauergasse, Kauergasse 3-5, 1150 Vienna.

CZECH, SLOVAK AND HUNGARIAN

CentroLING: Elective language courses in Czech, Slovak and Hungarian as first, second or foreign languages, are taught by native-speakers.

PRIMARY SCHOOLS:

* Dr. Bruno Kreisky Schule, Svetelskystraße 4-6, 1110 Vienna (Czech only)
* EPS Goldschlagstraße 14-16, 1150 Vienna
* GEPS Reisnerstraße 43, 1030 Vienna (Hungarian only)

SECONDARY SCHOOLS (LOWER-LEVEL):
* EMS 22 Anton-Sattler-Gasse 93, 1220 Vienna
* EMS Neustiftgasse 100, 1070 Vienna (Hungarian only)

NATIVE-LANGUAGE STUDY FOR FOREIGN STUDENTS

MUTTERSPRACHLICHER UNTERRICHT

Pupils attending Academic Secondary Schools ("AHS" p 125) whose mother tongue is not German or English are offered elective courses (*unverbindliche Übungen*) in their native language.

As of the 2019/2020 school year, the following languages are offered:

* Albanian
* Arabic
* Bosnian-Croatian-Serbian
* Bulgarian
* Chinese
* Czech
* Farsi
* Hungarian
* Italian
* Nepalese
* Polish
* Portuguese
* Romanian
* Russian
* Slovenian
* Spanish
* Turkish

Your child's school can provide information about locations and times.

Private
INTERNATIONAL
SCHOOLS

Private schools offering instruction in a foreign pupil's native language are an alternative to bilingual education in public schools, especially for families residing in Vienna for a short period only (e.g. diplomats). Such schools offer lesson plans similar to those in countries of origin and most issue an International Baccalaureate high school diploma (as opposed to the Austrian *Matura*).

SCHOOLS WITH ENGLISH AS PRIMARY LANGUAGE OF INSTRUCTION

* **Amadeus International School**
  Bastiengasse 36-38, 1180 Vienna.
  Kindergarten through high school, leading to International
  Baccalaureate diploma. Boarding and day students. Music and Arts Academy
  participation is optional

* **American International School (AIS)**
  Salmannsdorfer Strasse 47, 1190 Vienna.
  Not all AIS students are native-English speakers. Pre-school through high
  school leading to US high school diploma or International
  Baccalaureate diploma

* **Danube International School Vienna**
  Josef-Gall-Gasse 2, 1020 Vienna.
  Primary through high school leading to International Baccalaureate diploma

* **International Christian School Vienna**
  Wagramer Strasse 175 / Panethgasse 6a, 1220 Vienna.
  Denominational school with a US-based curriculum. Primary through high
  school leading to International Baccalaureate diploma

* **Mayflower Christian Academy**
  Fontanstraße 8, 1100 Vienna
  Denominational primary school and bilingual kindergarten, Arche Noah

* **Vienna Primary/European School (VES)**
  Lacknergasse 75 & Paulinengasse 16, 1180 Vienna.
  Kindergarten through high school leading to Austrian *Matura*
  Founded in 2001

* **Vienna International School (VIS)**
  Straße der Menschenrechte 1, 1220 Vienna.
  Primary through high school leading to International Baccalaureate diploma.
  Formerly known as the International Community School, which was founded
  under the patronage of the British, US and Indian Embassies when the army
  schools closed at the end of the allied occupation of Austria (1955).

The **US EMBASSY WEBSITE** lists international schools
in other Austrian provinces.

SCHOOLS WITH OTHER LANGUAGES OF INSTRUCTION

* **Lycée Francais**
  Liechtensteinstraße 37 A, 1090 Vienna.
  Kindergarten through upper-level secondary school

* **Japanese School**
  Prandaugasse 2, 1220 Vienna.

* **Swedish School**
  Scheibelreitergasse 15, 1190 Vienna.
  Kindergarten, pre-school and primary school

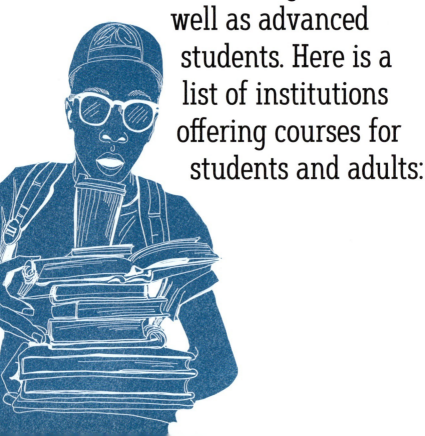

German courses for university students and adults

Language schools in Vienna offer German courses for beginners as well as advanced students. Here is a list of institutions offering courses for students and adults:

* **ACTILINGUA ACADEMY:** German courses (16+ years), summer school and holiday courses (12-19 years)

* **ADVENTUM INSTITUT:** German courses (14+ years)

* **ALINGUA CONCORDIS:** German courses (16+ years)

* **ALPHA SPRACHINSTITUT AUSTRIA:** German courses (14+ years), holiday courses (12-16 years)

* **BERLITZ:** German courses for young people and adults

* **DAS SPRACHENSTUDIO:** German courses (16+ years), German for pupils living in Vienna

* **DEUTSCH AKADEMIE:** German courses, summer courses (16+ years)

* **DEUTSCHINSTITUT:** German courses, summer courses (16+ years)

* **DEUTSCHOTHEK SPRACHSCHULE:** German courses, summer courses (16+ years)

* **DIALOG – DER SPRACHCAMPUS:** German courses (16+ years)

* **ELOQUENT SPRACHINSTITUT:** German courses (15+ years)

* **INNES VIENNA:** German courses, summer and winter school (16+ years)

* **INTERNATIONALES KULTURINSTITUT (IKI):** German courses, summer courses (16+ years)

* **LEARN QUICK:** German courses for young people and adults

* **LERNAKTIV:** German courses for pupils living in Vienna (6-18 years)

* **LOQUI SPRACH- UND BILDUNGSINSTITUT:** German courses (16+ years)

* **MERIDIAN SPRACHZENTRUM:** German courses (16+ years)

* **ÖJAP - ÖSTERREICHISCHE JUNGARBEITERINNENBEWEGUNG:** German courses (16+ years)

* **ÖSTERREICHISCHE ORIENT-GESELLSCHAFT:** German courses (16+ years)

* **SPRACHENZENTRUM DER UNIVERSITÄT WIEN:** German courses, summer intensive courses (16+ years)

* **VHS – WIENER VOLKSHOCHSCHULEN:** German courses (15+ years)

* **VORSTUDIENLEHRGANG:** German courses preparing international students for supplementary examinations

Life's too short to learn German*.

Don't be a stranger.

TESTIMONIALS

SANGITA, 51

Indo-German mother, born in Vienna, married to an Austrian

Growing up in Vienna, I attended both the English School (now renamed Vienna International School) and an Austrian public school, so I knew my children would thrive in the warmer, human atmosphere at VIS. Beyond having a diversity of nationalities and religions among the children and staff there, VIS focuses on developing worldly human beings instead of just forcing information into kids' brains. Classes are taught in English, but younger pupils are required to learn German and they can also study their own mother tongue there. There is a lot of turnover among the students, but this challenges pupils to adapt to unfamiliar social environments, and they'll remain open to new experiences and interactions for their entire lives.

CHRISTOPHER, 36,

native Viennese, attended American International School

My parents enrolled me at AIS starting in kindergarten. My brother and sister both graduated from there with Austrian *Matura* and American high school diplomas, but after a family crisis I transferred to a public *Gymnasium*. Once I left AIS, I realized that even as a native Wiener I never felt like one in that upper-class, international bubble. It was like being a third-culture kid without ever having left my hometown. AIS students don't even use public transportation to get to school – most of them commute on the school's own buses. Most of my international classmates never bothered to learn German. Though the AIS student body is not so diverse economically, I enjoyed the variety there in the sense that I learned with different sets of pupils in each course, unlike at public school where you sit in the same room with the same people all day.

KATHY*, 54

American citizen, married to an Austrian schoolteacher

I enrolled all three of my kids in the bilingual VBS class at a public primary school in an affluent neighborhood (lots of kids in designer clothes got dropped off in their parents' Porsches). The bilingual classes were more diverse than the rest of the school, because many of the parents are expats like me. VBS classes mix together English and German native pupils. Sometimes they were split up accordingly between the native Austrian and the English native speaker teachers. My kids and I found the Austrian teachers to be disinterested, passive-aggressive, and not at all creative, but we loved all of the native-speaker English teachers. All three kids turned out perfectly bilingual – it helped that they were conversant in both languages from the get-go.

SABINE, 45

English native speaker married to an Austrian

Born in Vienna, my daughters understood me when I spoke English to them at home, but neither spoke a word of English until just before they started their bilingual class at a public elementary school. We will definitely continue with the VBS system for *Gymnasium*. It would be silly not to take advantage of this free bilingual schooling. Of course, it is academically challenging, given that the children learn to read, write and do math in both German and in English. It's nothing the children can't handle. It's their "normal."

HELEN, 63

member of "U.S. Americans in Vienna" Facebook group

My son had a wonderful experience at [his bilingual public elementary school]. There weren't a lot of "native" English-speaking kids (those who spoke English at home) in the class, though. He started first grade with no German and by Christmas was speaking it very well. He got all ones there, but when he went to a regular public *Gymnasium* the German was a much higher standard and he struggled. Overall, the VBS experience is great for both kids and parents.

*name changed.

BRIAN, 36,
member of "U.S. Americans in Vienna" Facebook group

Having one child in a bilingual elementary school and another in a bilingual *Gymnasium*, I can say that if the parents understand a fair amount of German and are open to experiencing Austrian school culture, then the VBS route is the way to go. I've seen other non-Austrian parents who have a lot of difficulty – probably due to the culture clash and not being able to communicate in German. VBS is still a Viennese public school and is definitely more work for parents and students, but we've had mostly good experiences.

JONATHAN, 52
native English speaker working for an American firm in Vienna

Even though English is our mother tongue, when my wife and I relocated to Vienna we enrolled our two older children (aged 11 and 12) in normal Viennese public schools. None of them spoke a word of German beforehand, but kids are like sponges and they picked it up quickly. Later, we decided to send them to the American International School, because we found that its curriculum is more focused, its teachers more committed and it's generally better for less structured kids. Our youngest child learned German early in a *Kindergruppe* and now attends a public *Gymnasium*, but one with an all-day schedule and a progressive curriculum promoting tolerance.

GEORGE, 52

American expat married to a German, both bilingual

Our oldest daughter had already been in kindergarten in London when we moved to Vienna, but there were no issues when she transferred to one here, mainly because she was already bilingual – she had the advantage that her mom and our au pair in London are both German native speakers. In Vienna, we have had English native-speaker au pairs who have helped me teach English to our Vienna-born youngest daughter while she attended German kindergarten here.

SOPHIE, 48

Viennese, married to an English native-speaker

Though my husband spoke English with our daughter since her birth in Vienna, she rarely spoke it to us while she went to German-language kindergarten and elementary school. We applied for her placement in a bilingual DLP class at a public *Gymnasium* and were initially worried that she wouldn't pass the admissions interview (she did). During the summer before her first *Gymnasium* year, we vacationed in North America. By the time we came home she was suddenly speaking English like a native. She quickly made friends with other bilingual kids in her class (and we also became good friends with their parents). Unfortunately, the DLP wasn't offered in her upper-level *Gymnasium*, but by then she was completely fluent and comfortable in both German and English, and already moving on to French and Latin.

CHILDREN'S EDUCATION

Pre-school
KINDERGARTEN

INTRO

Parents of pre-school children in Vienna can choose from a wide array of options for day care, including public and private kindergartens, children's groups, child minders, and day care centers.

FORMS

PUBLIC *STÄDTISCHE*
kindergartens

The City of Vienna boasts 350 locations with some 28,600 available places for children up to 6 years of age. Vienna's public kindergartens are open year-round, except on official holidays, December 24 and December 31.

Attendance at public kindergartens is free of charge for all residents of Vienna, however there are modest charges for meals and special activities.

TYPES AND SIZES OF GROUPS

* Small children groups (*Kleinkindergruppen)* for infants up to age 3, no more than 15 children per group.

* Kindergarten groups (*Kindergartengruppen*) for ages 3 to 6, no more than 25 per group.

* Family groups (*Familiengruppen*) are smaller groups of up to 22 children of mixed ages (0-6). There are also family groups for ages 3 to 10, offering afternoon day care for school-age children.

Usually, each group is supervised by one teacher and one assistant. Groups integrating special needs children are smaller and have additional personnel.

SCHEDULES

You may enroll your child all day, part-day or half-day.

* All day: 6:30 to 17:30 (plus an extra half hour on either end, as necessary)
* Part-day: either 6:30 to 14:00, or noon to 17:30 (lunch included)
* Half-day: either 6:30 to noon, or 13:00 to 17:00 (no lunch included)

THERE ARE CURRENTLY FIVE KINDERGARTEN LOCATIONS OPEN UNTIL 20:00:

* *Landstraßer Hauptstraße 92-94, 1020 Vienna*
* *Mittelgasse 25, 1060 Vienna*
* *Laimäckergasse 18/1+2, 1100 Vienna*
* *Beingasse 19-21, 1150 Vienna*
* *Bernoullistraße 4, 1220 Vienna*

PRIVATE
kindergartens

Parents may opt for private pre-school programs, perhaps because their preferred public kindergarten has no available places available or they prefer foreign-language child care. The City of Vienna offers subsidies to parents who opt for private kindergartens (see p 82).

INTERNATIONAL /
ENGLISH-LANGUAGE

The pre-school age is a great time for children to learn a foreign language organically and most non-native kids have no problem adapting to a German or bilingual kindergarten environment. In certain cases, though, it may make more sense to enroll a child in a private English-language or bilingual program. Here are a few examples:

* **AMADEUS INTERNATIONAL SCHOOL**
* **AMERICAN INTERNATIONAL SCHOOL**
* **ARCHE NOAH** (bilingual, Christian)
* **THE CHILDREN'S HOUSE** (Montessori)
* **DANUBE INTERNATIONAL SCHOOL**
* **INTERNATIONAL MONTESSORI PRESCHOOL** (Montessori)
* **KINDEROASE** Weimarer Straße (bilingual, vegetarian)
* **UNITED CHILDREN** (bilingual)
* **VIENNA ENGLISH PRESCHOOL**
* **VIENNA INTERNATIONAL SCHOOL EARLY LEARNING CENTER/ GRADE PRIMARY**

In addition, there are children's groups (*Kindergruppen*), self-governed by parents, offering instruction (not by the parents) in English and other foreign languages (see below).

PRIVATE PRE-SCHOOLS
GERMAN-LANGUAGE

There are numerous other (too many to list here) private kindergartens and day care options (denominational and non-denominational). Many are grouped under governing associations (*Vereine*), which may receive higher subsidies from the City of Vienna.

DENOMINATIONAL
* **ST. NIKOLAUSSTIFTUNG ERZDIÖZESE WIEN**
* **VEREINIGUNG KATHOLISCHER KINDERTAGESHEIME**
* **DIAKONIE** (evangelical)
* **ISRAELITISCHE KULTUSGEMEINDE WIEN** (info on Judaic schools)

NON-DENOMINATIONAL
* **KINDERCOMPANY** (bilingual)
* **DACHVERBAND DER WIENER PRIVATKINDERGÄRTEN UND -HORTE**
* **VINDOBINI**
* **KINDER IN WIEN** (KiWi) (EN brochure)

Here's a city map showing all public and private child care locations:
https://bit.ly/2XvDAOm

SMALL-GROUP DAY CARE *TAGESELTERN*

An alternative to large-group kindergartens are small groups of up to five pre-school children cared for by a freelance "day mother" or "day father" (*Tagesmutter* or *Tagesvater*). The trained and licensed provider offers child care in his or her own home and organizes frequent excursions to local parks and playgrounds. If the group consists of Vienna residents receiving care at least 16 hours per week, the day parent receives subsidies from the City of Vienna making their services very affordable (from €20 to €90 per month, depending on the hours of care and not including meals). Without this subsidy, monthly costs can range from €288 to over €350.

THESE ASSOCIATIONS CAN HELP PARENTS FIND AND SECURE DAY PARENT PLACEMENT (PAID MEMBERSHIP REQUIRED):

* Tageselternzentrum
* Wiener Hilfswerk
* Volkshilfe Wien

CHILDREN'S GROUPS SELF-GOVERNED BY PARENTS

KINDERGRUPPEN

Another alternative to institutional pre-school child care, but one that requires significantly more parental involvement, are children's groups self-governed by parents *(Kindergruppen)*, which can cater to a wide range of specific pedagogic interests. A collective of parents forms the governing body and shares responsibilities for hiring professional staff, cooking meals, maintenance and administration.

Some groups cater only to infants up to age 3 *(Kleinkindergruppen)*, while others are "family"-like groups of up to 15 children of mixed ages.

In addition to committing their own time (about 15 hours per week), parents pay monthly dues (on average, about €100 per child for 40 care hours per week).

ASSOCIATIONS FOR CHILDREN'S GROUPS SELF-GOVERNED BY PARENTS:

* Verein der Wiener elternverwalteten Kindergruppen
* Verein Wiener Kindergruppen

AFTER-SCHOOL
DAY CARE *HORT*

Although the term *Hort* usually refers to after-school day care for school-age children, many pre-schoolers attend a *Hort* instead of, or in addition to, a kindergarten or children's group, especially during the compulsory kindergarten year (see below).

See p 81 for more information about *Horte*.

HOME CARE

While Austrian law mandates that a 5-year-old child must attend a kindergarten or children's group, exemptions are granted to parents who wish to care for their children at home and can prepare them for entry to primary school.
A child's parent must apply to the municipal department MA 11 for an exemption to the compulsory kindergarten year, or risk being fined (see p 123).

 Guidelines for home child care in the year before school entry (in German)

Online form to apply for exemption from compulsory kindergarten

INTEGRATIVE (SPECIAL NEEDS)

Whenever possible, the Vienna authorities want children with special needs to be enrolled in normal public kindergarten classes or in special integrated groups of a smaller size and additional personnel. If a child with special needs cannot meet the criteria for integration, there are special therapeutic public kindergartens (*heilpädagogische Sonderkindergarten*) available.

**CONTACT THE MUNICIPAL DEPARTMENT
FOR YOUTH AND FAMILY (MA 11)
INTEGRATION SECTION FOR CONSULTATION**

Rüdengasse 11, 1030 Vienna
+43 1 4000-90886 or -90889
fb-int@ma11.wien.gv.at

NEARLY 100,000 children in Vienna are in some sort of pre-school care (a third of them in public institutions).

ABOUT 44% of infants up to **2 YEARS OLD AND NEARLY 94% OF 3-TO-5-YEAR-OLD** children attend some form of day care.

Compulsory year
OF KINDERGARTEN
in Vienna

VERPFLICHTENDES KINDERGARTENJAHR

Children who have reached 5 years of age before September 1 and whose primary residence is in Vienna are obliged to attend a kindergarten or children's group *(Kinder-gruppe)* for at least 20 hours over at least four days per week.

Information folder in English (pdf download)

EXEMPTIONS FROM COMPULSORY PRESENCE IN KINDERGARTEN:

* During illness of child or parent
* During school vacations and up to five weeks of additional vacation
* Children who are cared for by a day parent *(Tagesmutter/-vater)* or who are raised at home (and do not need early-language support)
* Children receiving day care in another province
* Special-needs children
* Children admitted early to school

PENALTIES

Parents must inform the MA 11 of the exception in writing before June 30 (of the year the child must attend) or risk a fine of up to €440

 Online form

Finding
A PLACE

REGISTRATION

You may register your child for placement in a public kindergarten at any time, but registration during the main period (November-December) increases your chances of obtaining your preferred location (up to two can be requested). All registrations within the main period are given equal consideration.

MA 10 online registration form

For quicker registration outside of the main period, it is better to visit a **Kindergarten service point** or call +43 1 277 55 55. Bear in mind that placement options may be limited.

Once you register your child, he or she will receive a kindergarten identification number.

NOTE: Placement in a public kindergarten is not guaranteed! The following criteria are weighed by Vienna's municipal department for kindergartens (MA 10) in prioritizing placement:

CRITERIA FOR PREFERRED PLACEMENT IN PUBLIC KINDERGARTENS:

* Employment or academic schedule of parents (documentation required)
* Children with siblings currently attending school at the same location
* Social aspects (crisis situations)
* Proximity to residence
* Children aged 4 to 6 who have not attended kindergarten yet

If you are unable to secure a satisfactory public kindergarten placement for your child, you may opt for placement in a private kindergarten or children's group, a *Tageseltern* or an after-school day care center *(Hort)*.

To register your child for a private kindergarten, you must first apply for a customer number *(KundInnen-Nummer)* from the MA 10. With this number, you can apply directly to the private kindergarten. Each private kindergarten has its own application deadline and admissions policy, so it is a good idea to start your search a year before you plan to admit your child.

Download the application for a customer number (PDF)

An application can also be made in person at an MA 10 service point.

City Map showing all public and private child care locations **bit.ly/2XvDA0m**

Costs

If your child is a resident of Vienna, his or her attendance at a public kindergarten is cost-free; however, there are charges for meals and certain extras (e.g. extended attendance hours or special activities).

For non-residents, monthly costs *(Elternbeiträge)* range from about €160 - €270, depending on the number of attendance hours per day. These amounts are adjusted annually for inflation.

PRIVATE KINDERGARTENS, CHILDREN'S GROUPS & DAY CARE

Each private pre-school organization sets its own attendance fees; however, the City of Vienna applies parental subsidies (at least one parent must be a registered resident) which can entirely offset or reduce the expense. You must, however, apply for a customer number from the MA 10 (see p 81).

Subsidies are also available if your child attends an officially approved kindergarten at least 16 hours per week outside of Vienna. Depending on your child's age and the total hours of care he or she receives, you can be reimbursed for up to €270 of monthly care costs.

Download application for subsidies (PDF)

MEAL COSTS

While basic care at public kindergartens is free, part- or full-day attendance meals must be paid for *(Essensbeitrag)*. There are no meals with half-day attendance (8:00 – noon or 13:00 – 17:00). The current meal cost is €70 per month and is not tax-deductible.

SUBSIDIZED MEALS

The City of Vienna subsidizes meal costs for low-income families whose net monthly income is under €1,100. This also applies for children attending a private institution.

Info in English (PDF)

Online MA 11 application form

TAX DEDUCTIBILITY OF
PRIVATE CARE COSTS

Up to €2,300 in annual care costs for each child up to age 10 is a tax-deductible expense. However, costs related to outside courses, field trips, or entry tickets (e.g. for museums and theaters) are not deductible.

Some employers offer an annual tax-free "bonus" (up to €500) for child care.

NOTE: The prices shown above were valid at the date of publication. They are adjusted for inflation annually.

CARE DURING
VACATIONS AND HOLIDAYS

Public kindergartens are open year-round, except on official holidays, December 24 and December 31. Each location is allowed to close for up to three additional days per year (for pedagogic conferences). If child care is urgently needed on such days, a spot in a neighboring kindergarten may be available.

Private kindergartens may also close during school vacation weeks. Not all private day care centers offer vacation coverage. If no other day care options are available at their own institutions, children who attend private kindergarden or school may also enrol at a public after-school day care center (*Hort*).

See p 108 for more information on after-school day care and summer programs for children.

 Online searchable database of vacation camps and activities

Transition
TO PRIMARY SCHOOL

Austrian law requires all children who have turned 6 by September 1 to enter primary school. Some five-year-olds get bored with kindergarten and are already able to step up to the next level, while others may need more time to mature.

EARLY ADMISSION

VORZEITIGE AUFNAHME

If your child turns 6 after September 1 and before March 1, you may apply for early admission to primary school. The school will determine if the child is mature (*schulreif*) enough and has the necessary social skills. The public-school director may interview your child and determine whether he or she is eligible for early admission at the beginning of the school year.

COMPULSORY
PRE-SCHOOL

VORSCHULE

For children who are 6 on September 1, but who are not deemed fit for primary school (*schulreif*), there is a transition option for a pre-school year at a public or private institution. If a separate *Vorschule* class is not available, the pupil will be integrated into a standard 1st grade class.
In either case, a pupil has up to three years to complete the first basic level (*Grundstufe*, i.e. 1st and 2nd grades) of primary school.

See Page 104 for detailed information on admission to primary school

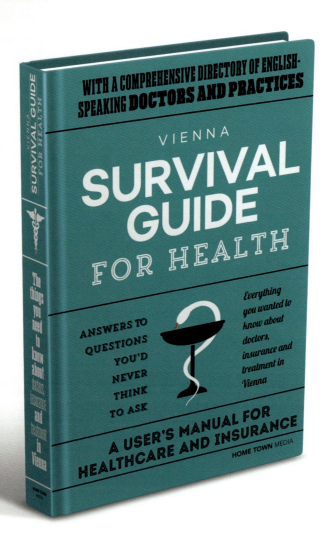

TESTIMONIALS

ALEX, 50,

native Austrian, mother of a child in a *Kindergruppe* 2012-2019

I enrolled my son in a "Kindergruppe" – an alternative child care option that is self-governed by parents – so that I could participate in his early development more than is possible at a public kindergarten. I was attracted by its smaller group size (no more than 14 kids per group), the close contact and collaboration between parents and professional staff, and being able to collaboratively shape the group's focus and rules.

Already at my first parents' evening, I became acquainted with other interesting and committed parents – even that mother obsessed with banning chocolate cereal at breakfast had her heart in the right place! Working collectively, we parents were responsible for managing, financing, cooking, cleaning, making repairs, communicating within the group, substituting for an ill child minder and (most importantly) attending the monthly parents' board meeting. Each parent commits a minimum of 15 hours per month. Those responsible for personnel management volunteer far more of their time.

At best, it was a utopian model of collective effort between parents, staff and children. At worst, it was a nightmare of collective crisis management. But if you have a strong desire to engage in your child's day care, the time to commit, and a disposition for collaboration, then a *Kindergruppe* is a great alternative to kindergarten or to home care.

SHAY, 46

British citizen who has lived in Vienna for 13 years

My children were born in Vienna and both attended a German-speaking private kindergarten followed by a bilingual (VBS) public primary school. At first, I was concerned by the fact that my children weren't taught to read in kindergarten like kids are in England. The emphasis here is on social interaction and education – lots of play, crafts, and off-site field trips. Although reading skills seem higher for many UK pupils my children's age, I believe this will even itself out once they reach secondary school. My children have an edge on their British peers in that they are learning in two languages, with excellent comprehension, verbal and written skills in both English and German.

GEORGE, 52

American expat married to a German, both bilingual

When it was time to place our oldest daughter in kindergarten, we did a lot of research first. Of course, proximity was a key factor – luckily our district (Währing) had great options. All-in-all, it went very well, but even though we secured a good spot, turnover in staff and care providers forced us to be vigilant. Parents need to stay involved in their kids' kindergarten and not just assume the plane flies on autopilot. You need to be proactive about things you feel strongly about, and you need to get other parents involved.

SOPHIE, 48

native Viennese, married to an English native speaker

When I returned to work after two years of maternity leave, I opted to obtain day care for my daughter with a *Tagesmutter*. I found one close to home who cared for a small group of 2 and 3-year-old girls in her own apartment. It worked really well from day one – it helped that we made a fun game out of the daily drop-off ritual. The *Tagesmutter* would always take "her" four kids out to a local playground for fresh air and exercise and serve them lunch. My husband, my father or I would pick my daughter up after her nap time and often it would be hard to get her to leave. After one and a half years with the *Tagesmutter*, my daughter was ready to go to a public kindergarten and her transition to a larger group of children was seamless.

Primary
School

VOLKSSCHULE

COMPULSORY SCHOOLING IN AUSTRIA
ALLGEMEINBILDENDE PFLICHTSCHULE OR APS

Austrian law requires all children who have turned six by September 1 to attend primary school. Compulsory schooling lasts through four (or five) years of primary school plus five additional years of secondary schooling (see Chapter 6) – typically pupils ages 6 to 15.

FORMS OF PRIMARY SCHOOL

PUBLIC PRIMARY SCHOOL *VOLKSSCHULE*

There are 288 primary schools in Vienna for more than 72,000 pupils. Four out of five are public schools.

AUSTRIA'S STATED GOALS OF PRIMARY SCHOOL EDUCATION ARE

* teaching cultural techniques (reading, writing, arithmetic)
* deepening children's understanding of their environment and helping them acquire and practice tolerance, participation, co-responsibility and respect for others

PUBLIC SCHOOL BASIC LEVEL 1 (*GRUNDSTUFE 1*)
1ST AND 2ND GRADES

Pupils have up to three years to complete this first basic level. Six-year-old pupils not yet deemed ready for school *(Schulreife)* may start with a pre-school *(Vorschule)* class or be required to repeat the 1st grade. Pupils can move up or down a level during the school year, upon recommendation by parents or teachers.

PUBLIC SCHOOL BASIC LEVEL 2 (*GRUNDSTUFE 2*)
THE 3RD AND 4TH GRADES OF PRIMARY SCHOOL.

SCHOOL HOURS

Public primary schools in Vienna have some flexibility to set their own schedules for classes, meals, learning, and free time. As a rule, the classroom lessons start at 8:00 and end before lunch, after which pupils may attend after-school day care, either on site or off (See Page 108).

EXPERIMENTAL SYSTEMS
SCHULVERSUCHE

Various school reform initiatives over the years have provided some public primary schools with leeway in how they organize themselves and what lesson plans are offered. This can take the form of separate pre-school classes, integrated multi-age classrooms *(Mehrstufenklassen)*, bilingual education (see p 42), and grouping of third and fourth graders according to performance levels.

 List of schools offering multi-age classrooms

Some public schools experiment with reform methods such as Freinet, Waldorf or Montessori-like "open learning" *(offenes Lernen)*, where pupils are assigned modular tasks that can be completed at a self-directed pace at learning stations.

PRIVATE &
DENOMINATIONAL
PRIMARY SCHOOL

Most private primary schools in Vienna are denominational (Catholic, Protestant, Judaic, Islamic), though not all of them restrict admissions to children within their respective religion. There are also non-denominational private schools offering alternative pedagogies (e.g., Montessori or Waldorf), as well as international schools offering lessons primarily in a foreign language *(see Bilingual & English-Language Schooling, p 42)* and elite schools such as the Theresianum.

HOMESCHOOLING & ALTERNATIVE SCHOOLS

PRIVATSCHULEN OHNE ÖFFENTLICHKEITSRECHT UND HÄUSLICHER UNTERRICHT

The Austrian law governing compulsory schooling makes an allowance for homeschooling *(häuslicher Unterricht)* or attendance at an unaccredited school *(Schule ohne Öffentlichkeitsrecht)*.

The process is not a simple one, however. As a parent, you must notify the Vienna Board of Education (Bildungsdirektion für Wien prev. Stadtschulrat) before the beginning of the compulsory school year. The Board will issue a positive judgement within a month if it can be reasonably certain that the alternative education is at least "of equal worth" to an accredited school.

At the end of each school year, your child must take an exam at an assigned public school to determine if he or she may continue with homeschooling. Failure to pass or to take the exam will result in your child having to repeat the grade level at an accredited school.

There is no charge for the application or testing; however, there is a small fee for an annual certificate of completion *(Jahreszeugnis)*.

(Additional info on p 142)

(Additional info on p 142)

wien.gv.at

CLASS
SIZES

Though public primary schools have some autonomy to determine class sizes, they are typically not larger than 25 students (the Austrian average is 18.8 students per class). Classes integrating special needs pupils are smaller and have teaching assistants.

Sizes of private school classes vary by institution.

DISCOVER ST. GILGEN INTERNATIONAL SCHOOL
AN INTERNATIONAL EDUCATIONAL EXPERIENCE IN A BREATHTAKING NATURAL SETTING

English. German. Russian. Spanish... Just a few of the languages that float down our hallways at **St. Gilgen International School**. Consisting of over 31 nationalities, our international school body is a diverse melting pot of talented students. Even more unique is our location – our school is nestled in the heart of a charming small town on the exquisite Wolfgangsee and surrounded by the Austrian alps. We are proud to offer our students full access to this outdoor paradise – the perfect natural environment for a world-class education.

In order to ensure every student flourishes at **St. Gilgen International School**, our philosophy of 'three pillars of excellence' applies to every child – excellence in education, care and activities. This means our highly qualified network of teachers, pastoral staff,nurses and outdoor trainers combine to ensure every student's talents are discovered, nurtured and developed.

Our promise is an education that is in fact a life-long love of learning. If you are interested in giving your child the gift of an international education, we invite you to experience it for yourself... We would be delighted to welcome you and your family to show the very best of what Austrian education offers. Simply visit us at **www.stgis.at** and set up your trial day!

"EVERY CHILD HAS TALENT AND ST. GILGEN INTERNATIONAL SCHOOL WILL DEVELOP IT"

SCAN ME

ADMISSION TO PRIMARY SCHOOL

The City of Vienna provides information about deadlines and required documents for registration in a primary school and for after-school day care (*Hort*, see p 74). Registration usually takes place in the fall and early winter of the year before admission.

A searchable database of all schools (*Schulführer*) is available online. It is also published in print format and available at all schools and service points.

 schulfuehrer.ssr-wien.gv.at/schoolguide/

Once you have chosen a preferred school, you must take your child with you there to register him or her and meet the school director, who will evaluate your child's readiness for admission *(Schulreife)* after consulting with you and your child's kindergarten teachers.

Your child must be deemed socially, emotionally, cognitively and physically able to attend primary school without being overwhelmed. Additionally, admission will be based upon his or her ability to satisfactorily communicate in German (if he or she is unable to do so, the school director can recommend special measures – See Chapter 3). Additional medical and psychological certifications may be requested.

When registering your child at a private school, it is advisable to meet with the school director well in advance of the registration deadline. Ensure that the private school you have selected has been accredited (that it is covered by *Öffentlicheitsrecht*), or you will need to apply for an exception to compulsory schooling (see Homeschooling, p 101).

EARLY ADMISSION *(VORZEITIGE AUFNAHME)*
If your 5-year-old child will turn 6 after the September 1 cut-off date, but before March 1 of the following year, you may apply for his or her early admission to primary school. The public school director will interview your child and determine whether he or she can be admitted at beginning of the school year.

PARENT–TEACHER MEETINGS *(ELTERNABENDE)*
Once your child is accepted, the school will typically invite parents to attend an orientation meeting prior to (or shortly after) the first day of school. Attendance is strongly recommended – if necessary bring an interpreter. In addition to receiving important information about the school and after-school day care, the assembled parents will usually elect a representative (*ElternvertreterIn)* who acts as a liaison between the school and parents.

FIRST DAY OF SCHOOL

In Austria, a child's first day of school is traditionally a major rite of passage and cause for celebration! The first "day" typically lasts an hour or so. It is customary that parents (and even grandparents) accompany their children into the classroom and then wait outside. When their children come out, Austrian parents typically present them with a *Schultüte* – a decorative, conical container filled with goodies and presents.

Beyond celebrating this important event in your child's life, it is also a good opportunity to meet other parents and school personnel.

Over the first week, more hours are added gradually to each school day until the normal schedule is reached.

AFTER- SCHOOL / EXTRACURRICULAR ACTIVITIES

Few public primary schools offer all-day instruction, but most offer lunch and after-school day care on site or at a nearby facility at quite reasonable prices (see Costs, p110 and p 111 for detailed information).

RELIGIOUS INSTRUCTION

"Reli," as most Austrian pupils call religion class, is a standard subject in Austria's compulsory public schools. As with other subjects, pupils are issued grades.

If your child has been registered in Austria as belonging to a state-recognized faith, he or she may take lessons in that faith. Most public primary schools offer classes in the Roman Catholic, Protestant, and Islamic faiths.

Religion classes are optional for pupils with no official religious confession *(ohne Bekenntnis)*. Until your child turns 14 years old, you must sign a waiver of religion classes within the first five calendar days of the school year.

COSTS

TUITION

Public primary school tuition is free for Vienna residents; however, there are modest fees for meals and afternoon day care (see p 174).

Private primary schools charge tuition fees that may or may not include meals and after-school day care, plus additional fees for registration, projects, supplies and field trips.

ESTIMATED ANNUAL COSTS FOR SOME PRIVATE SCHOOLS, INCLUDING AFTER-SCHOOL DAY CARE AND MEALS:

* **NEULANDSCHULE** (Catholic school in the 19th district): €4,500
* **THERESIANUM** (Elite school in the 5th district): €6,600
* **ASTRID LINDGREN ZENTRUM** (Montessori school in the 23rd district): €7,300
* **VIENNA INTERNATIONAL SCHOOL** (English school in the 22nd district): €18,500

PUBLIC AFTER-SCHOOL DAY CARE CENTERS

Monthly costs (*Elternbeiträge*) for public after-school day care centers (11:30 to 17:30, five days per week) are €176.73* per child per month. Meals cost €68.23* per child per month. Field trips, cultural events etc. cost extra. The costs also cover vacation day care.

Reduced costs for lower-income families are available under certain criteria (See p 174).

*prices adjusted annually to inflation index.

SUPPLIES
AND BOOKS

Schoolbooks are provided free of charge in public schools. Other school supplies (fountain pens, ink, writing utensils, art supplies, schoolbags, paper, notebooks, binders, compass, ruler, triangle, holepunch, glue, etc.) are not provided.

 wien.gv.at School materials (buying tips, in German)

schuleinkauf.at
Environmentally
sustainable supplies

PROJECT AND SPORTS WEEKS

Primary schools typically organize one or more multi-day field trips (usually for 3rd and 4th year pupils). Transportation, room and board for such trips is paid separately by the parents (in some cases subsidized by a school's parents association). Financial support for qualifying needy children is provided by the City of Vienna.

ASSESSMENT AND GRADES

THE STANDARD AUSTRIAN GRADING SYSTEM (*NOTENSKALA*) IS A FIVE-POINT SCALE:

* 1. Very good (*Sehr gut*)
* 2. Good (*Gut*)
* 3. Satisfactory (*Befriedigend*)
* 4. Sufficient (*Genügend*)
* 5. Insufficient (*Nicht genügend*)

Current law compels public primary schools to issue these grades only in the fourth school year, or if a pupil changes schools. Until then, alternative assessment techniques are allowed (e.g. verbal, written comments, self-evaluation, task journals…), as long as the class teacher and two-thirds of the parents agree to this.

Children whose German-language ability is judged insufficient are designated as so-called "non-regular pupils." During the two-year grace period they are given to learn basic German, they are not given grades (see p 44).

TRANSITION TO SECONDARY SCHOOL

FROM THE 4th INTO THE 5th SCHOOL YEAR

In the Austrian education system, decisions about your child's post-primary (secondary) education can be quite consequential, but they are not irreversible. For some expats living in Austria, it may seem a bit premature to make such important life decisions for a 10-year-old child!

Over the course of your child's primary school education, you will have ample opportunities with his or her teacher to discuss the best path forward. The school's decision to recommend a pupil for advancement to a **New Middle School (NMS)** or to a more academically selective Academic Secondary School (AHS) is based on the pupil's academic performance, social behavior, individual talents and interests. You and your child's primary school teacher will discuss the decision process and potential outcome during a parent-teacher evening or by special appointment *(Sprechstunde)*.

Before the end of the winter semester of the fourth school year, the primary school will provide you with an *Erhebungsblatt* with which you may register your child at a secondary school. In the second week of January, you must call your preferred secondary school to schedule a registration appointment for the registration week (usually the third week of February). You must take to that appointment the *Erhebungsblatt*, your child's winter semester report card and (for AHS schools only) a self-addressed, postage-paid A5 envelope. Some special schools (e.g. sports and bilingual schools) may have additional requirements for registration.

Around the Easter vacation (late March, early April), you will be notified by post or via your child's primary school whether your child has been accepted to the school.

See p 160 for specific secondary school eligibility and acceptance criteria

Is a child's educational path inherited?

There is ongoing debate about whether the educational background, occupation, social class and interests of a pupil's parents play a role in how a primary school makes its recommendati .ı for secondary school advancement.

Whether due to correlation or causation, it has been statistically ' ,wn that pupils whose parents have higher academic degrees are more l .y to attend an AHS, while pupils whose parents are in vocational trades a ,ikely to end up in an NMS, or vocational school.

An OECD (Organisation for Economic Co peration and Development) study also shows tha only 10% of Austrian schoolchildren whose parents ever com-pleted compulsory schooling have gor on to post-secondary (tertiary) studies – c y half the average of other industrialized coun ies. **Only 29% of working-age adults in Austria have ɔmpleted a level of schooling higher than that of tl ir parents**.

TESTIMONIALS

SOPHIE, 48,

native Viennese, married to an English native speaker

Because my daughter turned 6 years old in early September, she was not legally obligated to start elementary school that year, however she was already bored with kindergarten after spending 3 years there. I tried to enroll her at a bilingual public elementary school (VBS), but because there was so much demand there the school couldn't accept her until she turned 6. But a private German-language school correctly assessed her as *schulreif* and granted her early admission instead of waiting another year. It was the right decision and later she was accepted into a bilingual Gymnasium.

ALAN*, 51

American expat married to an Austrian, both bilingual

Our children have been enrolled in private Catholic elementary schools in Vienna since we moved here from London and (perhaps contrary to some other opinions we have read/seen along the way) we think these schools are great. Sure, they are traditional and have a religious component, which may not appeal to everyone. It always comes down to the school director, the specific teachers, and the amount of time you (as parents) invest in your child's education on an ongoing basis. Do your "homework": if you take the time to carefully research the school program and get to know the teachers and the school director, it can be a very positive and rewarding experience for parents and kids alike.

*name changed.

TEENAGER
EDUCATION

Secondary
SCHOOL

5th to 12th/13th school years; ages 10-19

The Austrian education system can be quite confusing to non-natives, especially at the secondary school level – a period when children's educational paths really begin to branch out. Get ready for an alphabet soup of acronyms (we will use the German abbreviations), and bookmark the overview chart (p 34) as it will help you navigate through it all!

The numbering of grade levels **restarts at "1"** at the beginning of secondary schooling. **"First class"** of secondary school is actually the **5th school year (including primary school).** To avoid confusion, we refer to grade levels by school year throughout this book.

Compulsory
SCHOOLING

Austrian law mandates five years of secondary schooling (typically pupils aged 10 to 15), i.e. through the 9th school year.

After the 9th school year, pupils can continue with a general academic education, pursue vocational training or forgo any further education.

FORMS
general education

After completion of primary school, a pupil is promoted to either an Academic Secondary School (AHS) or a New Secondary School (NMS). The latter must accept any pupil who has completed primary school, while the former can be more selective based upon academic performance.

AHS: ACADEMIC SECONDARY SCHOOL

ALLGEMEIN BILDENDE HÖHERE SCHULE

An AHS provides comprehensive and immersive education for academic-track pupils. The goal is the *Matura* diploma, which is required for university studies.

An AHS can be a public school or an accredited private school.

Commonly referred to as *Gymnasium,* an AHS consists of a four-year lower level (5th through 8th school years) and a four-year upper level (9th though 12th/13th school years). The upper level is comparable to college-prep high schools in the USA or to grammar school and sixth-form colleges in the UK.

LOWER LEVEL

UNTERSTUFE 5th - 8th SCHOOL YEARS

During the first two years of AHS (5th and 6th school years), all public *Gymnasia* offer nearly identical core lesson plans. In the 7th school year, an AHS' focus will diverge into one of the following strands:

* ***Gymnasium:*** Focus on languages (usually English, Latin and French), humanities and liberal arts

* ***Realgymnasium:*** Focus on math, science, linear drawing, technical/textile handwork

* ***Wirtschaftskundliches Realgymnasium:*** Focus on economics, business, technical/textile handwork

Some schools offer both *Gymnasium* and *Realgymnasium* in the same building or on the same campus.

Successful completion of the lower level entitles a pupil to advance to an upper-level AHS (most common), to a school for vocational education (BMS/BHS), or to a polytechnic school (PTS).

Celebrating 60 Years of Excellence!

Founded in 1959, The American International School · Vienna is the oldest English-language school in Austria, offering a unique combination of a nurturing, family atmosphere with a challenging educational environment backed by a longstanding tradition of academic achievement. School programs focus on academics, but also on the development of students' creative and leadership abilities and emotional intelligence.

AIS Vienna proudly serves around 800 students, representing over 60 countries, from Pre-Kindergarten through Grade 12 (IB Diploma or American Diploma). The school recognizes individual learning styles, making every effort to differentiate instruction, allowing students to reach their full potential in different areas, be it in academics, athletics, or in visual and performing arts.

Teachers at AIS are a dedicated group of educators who take a deeply personal interest in their students. The school is fortunate enough to include published authors, accomplished musicians and artists, and professional scientists among its faculty.

AIS' core values -- nurture, include, challenge and respect -- ensure that students develop intellectually and interculturally while internalizing the commitment and leadership necessary in today's globally-minded world.

Be part of **the story**!

Visit **www.ais.at** to learn more or call +43 1 401 32.

THE AMERICAN INTERNATIONAL SCHOOL · VIENNA · 1959-2019

SECONDARY SCHOOLING		COMPULSORY SCHOOLING	
		LOWER LEVEL	
AGE		10	11
SCHOOL YEAR		5	6
ACADEMIC SECONDARY SCHOOL (AHS)	GYMNASIUM	IDENTICAL CURRICULUM: (core subjects: German, English, math)	
	REALGYMNASIUM		
	WIRTSCHAFTS-KUNDLICHES REALGYMNASIUM		
NEW SECONDARY SCHOOL (NMS)		GENERAL BASIC EDUCATION Each school may place emphasis on: • Languages / humanities • Natural sciences / math • Economics / life skills • Music / creative skills • Sports	

*Some experimental upper-level Gymnasium are five-year programs
wien.gv.at/bildung/stadtschulrat/schulsystem/ahs/images/ahs-typen.gif

			UPPER LEVEL		
12	13	14	15	16	17/18
7	8	9	10	11	12/13*
Emphasis on language (Latin or French) and humanities		+ a third language (Latin or French) + *6 hours/week elective subjects*			
Emphasis on math, science, geometry, technical or textile crafts		+ Latin, French or Greek + *8 hours/week elective subjects*			
Emphasis on chemistry, technical or textile crafts		+ Latin, French or Greek; emphasis on psychology, philosophy, economics, business, and nutrition (includes an internship) +*8 hours/week elective subjects*			
Differentiation between basic and advanced studies		*NMS graduates may go on to upper-level Gymnasium or to a vocational school*			

UPPER LEVEL

OBERSTUFE 9th - 12th SCHOOL YEARS

With the successful completion of the 9th school year, a pupil has fulfilled his or her compulsory schooling; however, most AHS students will continue their upper-level schooling on the path toward a *Matura*.

Preparation for the *Matura* examination (*Reifeprüfung*)

Much of the upper-level AHS lesson plan is geared toward preparing pupils for the comprehensive *Matura* exams taken in the 12th school year. Passing the exam is a requirement for further academic study at university. (See *Reifeprüfung,* below)

Elective study (*Wahlpflichtfächer*)

Starting with the 10th school year, pupils may choose from elective courses and create an individualized lesson plan that furthers their specific academic and career goals. Depending on the type of *Gymnasium,* pupils take up to 10 weekly hours of elective study lessons (see diagram above).

Experimental classes

Any school may attempt to implement experimental pedagogical or organizational principles for individual classes or the entire school. Two-thirds of parents and teachers must approve the change and then the school board must also accept.

Some schools called *Oberstufenrealgymnasium* (ORG) offer only upper-level education (9th – 12th school years) and have a special focus, such as music, natural sciences, art/graphics, information technology and sport. Other special forms include bilingual Gymnasia (see p 42).

Successful completion (with *Matura*) of the upper-level AHS entitles pupils to enter a university, a university of applied sciences, a university/ college of teacher education, and post-secondary vocational courses, as well as trade apprenticeships or the workforce directly.

PRIVATE / PAROCHIAL AHS

International schools

Service offering consultation on Austria-wide choice of private schools and boarding schools privatschulberatung.at

BOARDING SCHOOLS (*INTERNAT*) IN VIENNA

* **AMADEUS INTERNATIONAL SCHOOL**
* **HIB-BOERHAAVENGASSE**
  (Public *Gymnasium* with music and arts emphasis)
* **BUNDESINTERNAT WIEN AM HIMMELHOF** (Age 10-19)
* **VIENNA BOYS' CHOIR SCHOOL**
* **CLARA FEY SCHULE** (for pupils with special needs)
* **BUNDES BILDUNGSINSTITUT** (Institute for the blind)

AFTER-SCHOOL DAY CARE

Each AHS is given leeway in setting its daily schedule for lessons. While there are some all-day schools *(Ganztagsschulen),* in most public AHSs afternoon day care *(Hort)* is optional and offered on site or at an external location. After-school day care typically combines time for studying (with or without tutoring), activities/clubs, and recreation, lasting until at least 16:00 and up until 17:30. Parents may opt for single days or full-week, but the decision must be made within the first week of the school year.

Monthly costs range from €26.40 (single day per week) to €88 (five days per week), plus extra for meals (if offered). Subsidies are available for needy families.

See p 172 for detailed information on after-school day care.

 metropole.city

AMADEUS International School Vienna is a unique day and boarding IB World School with an integrated Music and Arts Academy.

We are dedicated to creating an internationally minded community of happy, passionate, and aspirational learners.

Through a caring, individualized approach, we develop curiosity, creativity, and excellence.

Come visit our campus!
PREMIUM BOARDING and AMADEUS MUSIC and ARTS ACADEMY

Bastiengasse 36-38, 1180 Vienna | Austria, **www.amadeus-vienna.com**

NMS: NEW SECONDARY SCHOOL *NEUE MITTELSCHULE*

Formerly known as *Hauptschule*, an NMS is a public school spanning the 5th through 8th school years. While an AHS can reject an applicant due to poor academic performance in primary school, an NMS accepts all pupils who have completed the 4th year of primary school with a grade of at least "sufficient."

NMS prepares pupils for future vocational training according to individual interests, abilities, disposition and skills. NMS graduates can go on to intermediate or higher vocational schools (see BMS and BHS, below), or to an upper-level AHS (9th to 12th or 13th school years).

Beginning with the 7th school year, NMS pupils pursue advanced lessons in German, math and foreign language (similar to AHSs) or they receive basic instruction, depending upon each pupil's interests and career goals.

A special school form, the *Wiener Mittelschule* (WMS), is found in some NMS and AHS locations. It provides additional emphasis on learn-coaching, native-speaker teachers, elective courses and Europass training (development of career portfolio/CV to facilitate European interaction between jobseekers and employers).

NMS WITH SPECIAL FOCUS
SCHWERPUNKTSCHULEN

Examples of different focuses include ecology, music, creativity, natural history, foreign languages, information technology, sport, health and nutrition.

The so-called *Sportmittelschule* is a sport-focused NMS that also includes the compulsory 9th school year.

A sport- or music-focused NMS has additional admissions criteria (auditions, medical certification etc.).

SPECIAL NEEDS SCHOOLS
SONDERSCHULE

Whenever possible, special-needs children are integrated into normal school classes and are supported by additional class assistants. For some especially needy pupils, or for those finding it challenging to integrate into a normal school environment, there are nine types of special needs schools in Vienna.

VOCATIONAL TRAINING

VOCATIONAL TRAINING IN AUSTRIA: THE BASICS

You want to be an office clerk, a cook, or an electrical technician? The good news is that Austria's education system offers you three main ways to acquire vocational training: the dual vocational education and training (VET) program *(duale Berufsausbildung),* and two predominantly school-based programs. The features of each are further explained below.

A list of all vocational schools in Vienna can be found here:

abc.berufsbildendeschulen.at

APPRENTICESHIPS *LEHRE*
WITHOUT AND WITH *MATURA*

NMS as well as lower-secondary AHS graduates desiring to learn a profession who have finished their eighth year of education need to spend one final year at a pre-vocational school *(Polytechnische Schule)* to wrap up nine years of compulsory schooling. Pupils also have the option to voluntarily attend the pre-vocational school for two years to receive an extra year of education. At the pre-vocational school, pupils are familiarized with a selection from around 200 available apprenticeships through visits to companies and training workshops. The training professions include, for instance, construction, administration and organization, engineering, graphics, commerce, and fashion. (You can find a complete list of all apprenticeships here: **bmdw.gv.at).** The curriculum also comprises general education and

 fundamental vocational education in areas of interest to the individual pupil. Pupils with special educational needs can attend integrated classes.

Upon completion, pupils who want to continue with a more school-focused approach can transfer to the second year of a school for intermediate vocational education (*BMS,* see p 138) or to the first year of a school for higher vocational education (*BHS,* see p 140). Alternatively, they can start an apprenticeship in the form of a dual vocational education and training program, which is explained in more detail below.

The dual vocational education and training (VET) program, in essence apprenticeship training, is a popular way of gaining vocational training in Austria. To be admitted, pupils must have signed a vocational training contract. In the course of the VET program, pupils spend 80% of their time being trained at a company, while the remaining 20% are devoted to deepening their general education as well as acquiring work-relevant

theoretical knowledge at a vocational school. The apprenticeship training typically lasts two to four years. It concludes with an a practical apprenticeship-leaving examination. Upon successful completion, graduates can attend a Master Craftsman School (Meisterschule), which offers specialized courses to further deepen their theoretical and practical education. Graduation from these schools includes a mastership exam (Meisterprüfung). You can find more information on the dual vocational education here:

 apprenticeship-toolbox.eu.

Another great opportunity is the apprenticeship-with-*Matura* model (*Lehre mit Matura*). It allows pupils to prepare for and partly take the *Matura* exams during their apprenticeship training. The apprenticeship-Matura (see *Berufsmatura* or *Berufsreifeprüfung*, p 152) consists of four exams in German, math, a modern foreign language and a specialist area. The training institution and the pupil can choose if and how the *Matura* preparations are integrated within the vocational training. In Vienna, the institution responsible for *Lehre mit Matura* is the Informations-, Beratungs- und Koordinationsstelle des Kultur- und Sportvereins der Wiener Berufschulen (see p 267).

SCHOOL FOR INTERMEDIATE VOCATIONAL EDUCATION *BMS*

Another way to acquire professional skills is by attending a three- or four-year school for intermediate vocational education (*Berufsbildende mittlere Schule,* or *BMS*). These schools combine basic work-related competences, such as accounting or business studies, with a general education, but they don't include a higher education entrance exam. Pupils are often encouraged or required to complete practical training or internships.

Individual BMSs have one of various specializations, for instance technical skills/commerce/crafts, business and economics, fashion, the hotel and restaurant industry/tourism, social professions, sports, social care/healthcare/nursing, agriculture/forestry, and social services. Prerequisites for admission are eight years of compulsory schooling and, in some cases, the passing of an entrance exam. The *BMS* program concludes with a final exam.

Upon completing the *BMS*, pupils can work in their area of specialization, but they can also continue their education with advanced training courses (*Aufbaulehrgänge*) which may lead to the diploma exam (*Diplomprüfung*). Alternatively, after further training courses, they can take the higher education entrance examination
(see *Berufsreifeprüfung*, p 152).

VOCATIONAL EDUCATION IN HEALTHCARE: NURSES, MASSEURS AND MEDICAL TECHNICIANS

Nurse training is currently changing in Austria. As of 2024, schools for healthcare and nursing (*Schulen für Gesundheits- und Krankenpflege*) will still offer a three-year training program in qualified nursing care. Admission prerequisites include 10 years of schooling and the successful completion of an admission interview and/or test. The schools usually cooperate with hospitals, which provide vocational education. At the end of the training, pupils write a thesis and take a diploma exam. Qualified nurses can take up employment, take the higher education entrance examination (see *Berufsreifeprüfung,* p 152), or complete advanced training to prepare for leadership roles or to specialize in children's/youth care or psychiatric health. After 2023, the schools for healthcare and nursing will offer training in assistant nursing only, while training in qualified nursing will be transformed into a bachelor's degree at universities of applied sciences (see university of applied sciences, p 211).

If you are interested in becoming a medical masseur or medical technician, you have the choice between different training programs, some of which are organized in association with hospitals. Admission requirements differ in each case. You can find more information here:

 sozialministerium.at

SCHOOL FOR HIGHER VOCATIONAL EDUCATION *BHS*

Another vocational training option is a five-year school for higher vocational education (*Berufsbildende höhere Schule,* or *BHS*). The *BHS* offers higher-level vocational training plus a comprehensive general education. Different types of *BHS* have their own names: the higher technical education institute (*Höhere technische Lehranstalt,* or *HTL*) specializes in technology, engineering, or industrial design, the higher economic education institute (*Höhere Lehranstalt für wirtschaftliche Berufe,* or *HLW*) focuses on economics, communication, design and fashion, tourism, nutrition and administration, while business academies (*Handelsakademie,* or *HAK*) teach accounting and business administration. (Further available specializations include forestry, childhood pedagogy).

The main advantage of the *BHS* is that it combines job training (also through obligatory internships and training within firms) with a higher education entrance exam.

Prerequisites for admission to a BHS are the successful completion of at least eight years of compulsory schooling. In some cases, the admission procedure includes an entrance exam. Pupils conclude their BHS education with a combination of a higher education entrance examination *(Reifeprüfung),* plus a certificate granting direct access to legally regulated professions (*Diplomprüfung). BHS* graduates can seek immediate employment in a specialist area, study at a university, or start their own business. This list of Viennese schools (ordered by district) also lists *BHSs* and *BMSs.*

meinbezirk.at

COLLEGES *KOLLEGS*

If you have attended an *AHS* but want to additionally acquire vocational training, then a college *(Kolleg)* might be a suitable option. These four- to six-semester courses (depending on whether the course is full-time or consists of evening classes) are offered by some *BHSs*. There are colleges focusing on technology, arts and crafts, commerce, trade, elementary or social pedagogy, fashion, tourism, and economics. The admission criterion is that you have passed a school-leaving examination *(Reifeprüfung,* see p 146), vocational matriculation examination *(Berufsreifeprüfung,* see p 152) or a limited education entrance examination *(Studienberechtigungsprüfung,* see p 250) - for technical colleges, having completed a four-year technical course is often sufficient. College graduates do not receive a bachelor's degree, but they pass a diploma examination that grants them certain rights according to trade regulations in the respective profession. You can find a list of colleges in Vienna here:

wien.arbeiterkammer.at (download PDF in German).

BILINGUAL
VOCATIONAL SCHOOLS

The vast majority of vocational schools in Austria teach in German. However, there are bilingual schools (German and English), such as the International Business College Hetzendorf (a HAK)

ibc.ac.at

and schools with bilingual classes,
such as the HTL Spengergasse

spengergasse.at.

HOMESCHOOLING /
UNACCREDITED SCHOOLS
SCHULE OHNE ÖFFENTLICHKEITSRECHT

The Austrian law governing compulsory schooling makes an allowance for homeschooling *("häuslicher Unterricht")* or attendance at an unaccredited school *("Schule ohne Öffentlichkeitsrecht")*.

The process is not a simple one, however. As a parent, you must notify the Vienna Board of Education (Bildungsdirektion für Wien, prev. Stadtschulrat) before the beginning of the school year. The Board will issue a positive judgement within a month if it can be reasonably certain that the alternative education is at least "of equal worth" to a standard school. It will also provide information about the necessary external exams your child must pass *(Externistenprüfungen)* to complete compulsory schooling, be admitted into an accredited school or to become eligible to take the comprehensive equivalency exams *(Externistenreifeprüfungen)*.

Failure to pass, complete or submit the results of the external exams for compulsory grade levels (through the 9th school year) results in the pupil being required to attend an accredited school the following year (repeating the same school year). Failure to complete or submit the results may also result in fines for the parents/guardians.

There is no charge for the application or testing; however, there is a €14,30 fee for an annual certificate of completion *(Jahreszeugnis)*.

RELIGIOUS COMMUNITY
SCHOOLS
JUDAIC & ISLAMIC

Attendance at a religious community school may not fulfill Austria's compulsory education requirement. If the school is not accredited (*ohne Öffentlichkeitsrecht),* pupils are subject to the same regulations as homeschooled children *(see above).*

The following associations provide advice and listings for Judaic and Islamic private schools in Vienna.

 Israelitische Kultusgemeinde Wien
ikg-wien.at

 Islamische Glaubensgemeinschaft in Österreich
derislam.at

(Additional info on *Externisten,* p 150)

HIGHER EDUCATION entrance examinations

Several educational paths in Austria lead to higher (tertiary) education, all involving entrance examinations. The most common ticket to higher academic study is the Secondary School Leaving Certificate, or *Matura*.

ZENTRAL*MATURA*

REIFEPRÜFUNG / DIPLOMPRÜFUNG

The comprehensive *Matura* exams were standardized nationally as of the 2014/2015 school year and now employ a three-pillar model (*Drei-Säulen-Modell*).

PILLAR 1: THESIS AND PRESENTATION

VORWISSENSCHAFTLICHE ARBEIT, PRÄSENTATION UND DISKUSSION – VWA (FOR AHS CANDIDATES)

Pupils decide on a theme in the first semester of the 11th school year and have until the beginning of the final semester of the final year to deliver a presentation to the examination commission (*"Prüfungskommission"*).

* The VWA consists of a written thesis, a presentation of the thesis and subsequent discussion.
* If a VWA receives a failing grade, the pupil must try again with a different topic.

DIPLOMARBEIT (FOR BHS CANDIDATES)

Pupils must write a thesis on a professional or occupational issue and present it orally. Topics are chosen with an adviser and ideally groups of two to five students work in teams on the thesis and presentation. Teams and topics are fixed by the beginning of the final school year. The thesis must be submitted no later than four weeks before the proctored exams are taken (see below).

PILLAR 2: PROCTORED EXAMS
KLAUSURPRÜFUNGEN

Pupils must sit three or four written exams in German, math, and at least one living language (English, French, Italian, Spanish). Latin and ancient Greek are not compulsory, but may be required for some areas of advanced study.

Elective non-standardized exams are also possible in other subjects (other living languages, physics, music, geometry etc.).

Written exams with a failing grade must be repeated. It is possible to retry with oral exams *(Kompensationsprüfungen)*.

PILLAR 3: ORAL EXAMS
MÜNDLICHE PRÜFUNGEN

Oral exams are not centralized but are instead administered by each school individually, according to its own emphases. Pupils may take either two or three oral exams.

THREE-PILLAR MODEL

1

THESIS AND PRESENTATION

FOR AHS CANDIDATES

Vorwissenschaftliche Arbeit Präsentation und Diskussion (VWA)

The *VWA* consists of:

* a written thesis
* presentation of the thesis
* subsequent discussion of the thesis

Candidates decide on a theme in the first semester of the 11th school year and have until the beginning of the final semester of the final year to write the thesis and deliver a presentation to the examination commission (*Prüfungskommission*).

FOR BHS CANDIDATES

Diplomarbeit

Two to five students work in teams on a written thesis about an occupational issue and present it orally.

Topics are chosen with an adviser and are fixed by the beginning of the final school year.

The thesis must be submitted no later than four weeks before the proctored exams are taken.

If a VWA or *Diplomarbeit* receives a failing grade, the pupil must try again with a different topic.

2	**3**
PROCTORED EXAMS	**ORAL EXAMS**

FOR ALL CANDIDATES	
Klausurprüfungen	*Mündliche Prüfungen*
Three required written exams * German * Math * At least one living language (English, French, Italian, Spanish)	Two required exams Oral exams are not centralized but are instead administered by each school individually, according to the school's own emphases. Each exam lasts about 10-15 minutes. Only one question is asked.
OPTIONAL FOURTH EXAM	**OPTIONAL THIRD EXAM**
Elective non-standardized exams are also possible in other subjects (other living languages, physics, music, geometry etc.) Latin and ancient Greek are not compulsory, but may be required for some areas of advanced study. If a fourth written exam is taken, the candidate only takes two oral exams. Written exams with a failing grade must be repeated. This is possible through an oral exam. ("*Kompensationsprüfungen*").	Candidates may take a total of either two or three oral exams. Make-up exam policies are decided by each school autonomously.

HIGHER EDUCATION ENTRANCE EXAMINATION FOR EXTERNAL STUDENTS

EXTERNISTEN REIFEPRÜFUNG

Pupils attending private schools with or without accreditation, as well as pupils who are homeschooled, must also take the *Reifeprüfung* to gain admission to higher academic studies. However, the exams must be taken in accordance with the external testing method (see p 249).

AN EXTERNAL EXAM IS ALSO NECESSARY FOR PUPILS:

* who have completed only compulsory schooling
* whose foreign diploma was not recognized or given equivalence (see p 154 on *Nostrifikation)*
* who did not pass or take the exam while attending a public AHS

REQUIREMENTS

Pupils must have completed eight years of compulsory schooling, without failing any or having any missing marks in the compulsory subjects (German, math, English). Make-up exams *(Zusatzprüfungen)* in specific subjects are possible.

CERTIFICATION EXAMS *(ZULASSUNGSPRÜFUNGEN)*

Before external candidates take the Reifeprüfung, they must take certification exams in each subject (based upon the complete lesson plans of upper-level *AHSs/Gymnasiums*). The order and timing of each exam may be chosen by the candidate pupil. There are no set requirements for exam preparation. Candidates may study independently, with tutors, in private schooling, through test prep courses, etc.

Pupils must apply to the AHS examination commissions *(AHS-Prüfungskommissionen)* for permission to take the exams. (Cost: €14.30 + €3.90 for each document submitted. Costs are waived for homeschooled pupils). Once the commission has issued its allowance decree *(Zulassungsdekret),* a date for the examination may be set.

GENERAL HIGHER EDUCATION ENTRANCE EXAMINATION

BERUFSREIFEPRÜFUNG – BRP

The BRP *(Berufsmatura* or *Lehre mit Reifeprüfung)* is a required higher-education entrance examination for pupils who have successfully completed an initial vocational education (BMS/VET etc.) and vocational apprenticeships. It combines the practicality of a vocational education with the benefits of a *Matura.*

THE EXAM CONSISTS OF FOUR PARTS: German, math, a modern foreign language, and one specialist area relating to the relevant vocational education. With the exception of math, all exams comprise both written and oral components. The four exams may be taken together or separately but may not be completed before the pupil is 19 years old. A pupil may not begin to take the exam until he or she has applied to a public upper level secondary school *(AHS)*.

The exam can be prepared for independently, through distance learning or with preparatory courses (some of which are free of charge to pupils already in vocational training). If the preparatory course is taken at a certified learning center, up to three exam segments may be taken there; however at least one must be taken at an external public school.

In addition to granting access to all forms of Austrian higher education (universities, colleges, academies, and post-secondary vocational courses), a successfully taken BRP also allows entry into higher levels of civil service in the federal government.

RECOGNITION OF FOREIGN CERTIFICATES and diplomas
Nostrifikation

A certificate or diploma issued by a foreign school (or a school with foreign lesson plans within Austria) may require official comparison and alignment with Austrian standards to meet qualification requirements for higher education entrance examinations.

UP TO THE 8th
SCHOOL YEAR
LOWER-LEVEL AHS

The Vienna Board of Education (Bildungsdirektion für Wien) decides if the foreign certificate allows a pupil to undergo the *Externistenreifeprüfung*.

The original certificate (and a certified translation if it isn't in German) must be presented.

If the level of German study is judged insufficient or is nonexistent, the pupil must pass an external exam *(Sprachbeherrschungsprüfung)* to ascertain whether he or she has the German-language skills required for the 8th school year. Additional requirements may be requested.

FROM THE 9th
SCHOOL YEAR
UPPER-LEVEL AHS

The Austrian Federal Ministry of Education, Science and Research (Bundesministerium für Bildung, Wissenschaft und Forschung) is the entity responsible and determines if any further examinations are necessary.

For detailed information on nostrification, see p 224.

Studying
ABROAD

Several private organizations offer foreign-exchange and study-abroad programs for secondary school pupils aged 12-18. Most programs will let you choose a destination country, but not necessarily a specific location or institution. It is also permissible to organize these independently; however, you are responsible for obtaining any required visas, insurance and living expenses.

Pupils can study abroad for a semester or for a year or they may attend summer school or other study programs of shorter duration. Pupils may live with a host family or at a boarding school.

Application deadlines vary depending on the organization, are but generally six to nine months before travel is planned. Passing grades as well as good physical and mental health are prerequisites for participation.

Costs are generally high for secondary school programs (there are less-expensive alternatives during tertiary education); however, stipends and grants are available based on merit or need. If a pupil is placed in a private school, tuition fees may be supplemental to the program fees.

It is recommended that you check with the Austrian tax and revenue authority (Finanzamt) to see if family benefits (Familienbeihilfe) will still be received if your child studies abroad for more than six months in a tax year.

For study abroad lasting at least five months but no longer than one school year, a certificate from the host school counts as the equivalent of attendance at a domestic school and no external exams are required. Upon returning from abroad, pupils should be promoted to the next higher level, but it is advisable to confirm this in advance with the pupil's school director.

ONLINE LISTING OF AGENCIES AND PLATFORMS

 wienxtra.at

ADMISSION
to secondary
SCHOOL

Before the end of the first semester of the fourth school year (final year of primary school), you and your child should have visited and selected some preferred schools. Registration for public secondary schools begins after the semester break (in February).

Primary schools will provide you with information (*Erhebungsblatt*) about your child's promotion into secondary school.

THE VIENNA SCHOOL BOARD ISSUES ITS DECISION ABOUT WHICH PUBLIC SCHOOL YOUR CHILD WILL ATTEND BASED ON SEVERAL FACTORS:

* Location: Preference will be given to schools close to your residential address. Your child is guaranteed placement in a nearby public school, but not at schools outside of your immediate area.

* Grades: Passing grades in primary school are required for entry into all public secondary schools. AHS schools have stricter criteria than NMS schools – grades lower than a "Good" (2) in the subjects of German, reading, writing and math are usually disqualifying unless the primary school makes an exception and nonetheless certifies the pupil as ready for an AHS school (see below).

* Siblings: Children with older siblings already attending the preferred school usually have a better chance of admission.

Near the end of the fourth school year, primary schools issue a certificate (*Aufnahmebestätigung*) confirming that the pupil has met all of the requirements for promotion to either an NMS or an AHS.

Special requirements for admission to lower AHS years (starting with 5th school year)

Nearly half of all Vienna's primary school pupils will go on to attend an AHS. Pupils must have received "very good" (1) or "good" (2) marks in the compulsory subjects *(Pflichtfächer)*: German, reading, writing and math, and passed all other subjects for the final year of primary school. If a pupil has been given a "satisfactory" (3) grade in one or more of these subjects, the primary school may nevertheless agree to certify that he or she is promotable, based on other academic factors and the primary's school's confidence that the child will be able to handle instruction at an AHS.

If a pupil does not meet the above criteria – or if a pupil has been schooled at home or in schools without public accreditation – he or she may take an entrance exam (*Aufnahmeprüfung*) at the preferred AHS, as long as he or she has passed all primary school subjects in external exams. The AHS entrance exams are on Tuesday and Wednesday of the final week of the school year.

Because of high demand, some AHS have even stricter academic criteria for selection, particularly for non-local students. Special schools (e.g. bilingual schools, music and sport schools) have additional admissions criteria and may require an entrance exam or interview.

PRIVATE SECONDARY SCHOOLS

Each private secondary school has its own admissions criteria and dates for registration. Contact each school's direction well in advance of deadlines for information.

ADMISSION REQUIREMENTS FOR UPPER AHS YEARS OR ORG (STARTING WITH 9th SCHOOL YEAR)

Pupils who have successfully passed their 8th school year, whether at an AHS, NMS, FMS, or PTS, may apply for admission to the upper-year AHS level.

An entrance exam may be required if the previous lower-year AHS school curricula have not comprised enough required courses, if pupils' marks are below average, or if pupils have received schooling at home or from unaccredited private institutions.

Each AHS decides if a pupil is admitted. At this level, placement preference is not necessarily given to pupils living close by.

What skills does a student need

to be successful

in the future?

HOW DOES *the Future* LOOK?

As a society we are facing unprecedented challenges – social, economic and environmental – driven by accelerating globalisation and a faster rate of technological developments. At the same time, those forces are providing us with a myriad of new opportunities for human advancement. The future is uncertain and we cannot predict it; but we need to be open and ready for it. The students entering school this year will be young adults in 2030 and we need to recognise that we are preparing them for jobs that have not yet been created, technologies that have not yet been invented, to solve problems that have not yet been anticipated. This reality provides a shared responsibility to seize opportunities and find solutions.

What skills SHOULD A STUDENT DEVELOP TO BE SUCCESSFUL IN THE FUTURE?

To navigate through such uncertainty, students will need to develop curiosity, imagination, resilience and self-regulation; they will need to respect and appreciate the ideas, perspectives and values of others; and they will need to cope with failure and rejection, and be confident to move forward in the face of adversity. Their motivation will be more than getting a good job and a high income; they will also need to care about the well-being of their friends and families, their communities and the planet.

HOW DOES VIENNA INTERNATIONAL SCHOOL APPROACH LEARNING TO BEST MEET the needs of a 21st century student?

In the face of an increasingly volatile, uncertain, complex and ambiguous world, schools can make a difference as to whether people embrace the challenges they are confronted with or whether they are defeated by them. In an era characterised by a new explosion of scientific knowledge and a growing array of complex societal problems, it is appropriate that curricula and learning environments should continue to evolve, perhaps in radical ways. The strategic intents of Vienna International School are designed to equip learners with competencies they need, to shape their own lives and contribute to the lives of others. We use our International Baccalaureate

curriculum to help every learner develop as a well-rounded person, fulfil his or her potential and help shape a shared future built on the well-being of individuals, communities and the planet. Our youngest learners are already very clear about the need to abandon the notion that resources are limitless and there to be exploited; they value common prosperity, sustainability and well-being. They are championing an agenda in support of the need to be responsible and empowered, placing collaboration above division, and sustainability above short-term gain.

Who is VIENNA INTERNATIONAL SCHOOL?

Vienna International School (VIS) is a three-programme school (International Baccalaureate continuum school), hosting 1400 students from 111 nationalities, with ages between 3 and 18 years of age. The school has assembled a team of 267 highly professional staff committed to providing its students an education that is inspiring, inquiring and involved in a truly inclusive environment. The School has recently gained significant recognition for its work in developing a sustainable development agenda, being accredited as the first Eco School International in Austria, by three international institutions (Eco Schools, Global Schools & Umweltzeichen).

www.vis.ac.at

COSTS

TUITION

Public secondary schools don't charge tuition; however, after-school day care, class trips and special activities cost extra.

Private school tuition fees vary with each school. Most charge a non-refundable application fee. If a pupil is accepted, it is also possible that a non-refundable deposit is required to hold his or her place. Some schools offer discounted tuition and fees for enrollment of additional siblings.

PROJECT AND SPORT WEEKS

Most schools organize multi-day class trips centered around, for example, skiing, sports, and language. These carry extra costs but may be subsidized with parent organization (*Elternverein*) funds. Participation is mandatory, as such weeks are considered a part of school instruction. If a pupil has a good excuse not to participate in overnight trips outside of the city with the class, an exception may be made, but the pupil must attend an alternative class.

Subsidies for school events lasting five days or more are available for low-income families. Information is available at each school.

GRADING

Grading is generally based on test results, attendance, class participation, timeliness, homework completion, papers/ presentations/reports, special projects, and behavior. Grades are issued at the end of the winter semester (*Semesterzeugnis*) and for the full school year (*Jahreszeugnis*).

Grades at AHSs are on a five-point scale

1. Very good (*Sehr gut*)
2. Good (*Gut*)
3. Satisfactory (*Befriedigend*)
4. Sufficient (*Genügend*)
5. Insufficient (*Nicht genügend*)

At NMSs, the same scale is used. Starting with the 7th school year, however, pupils can opt for basic or advanced instruction in core subjects (German, math and English). Pupils who opt for basic instruction receive only pass/fail grades but may not advance to higher school levels after their compulsory education is complete.

EARLY WARNING SYSTEM
FRÜHWARNSYSTEM

The goal of the early warning system is to notify parents that a pupil is in danger of receiving a failing grade or has behavioral problems. Participation in a consultation meeting with the teacher is compulsory for the pupil and parents so underlying causes may be identified and preventive measures (e.g. tutoring, individualized instruction plan, German-language classes, and remedies for learning weaknesses) may be proposed.

TESTIMONIAL

SOPHIE, 48

native *Wienerin*, married to an English native speaker

Throughout my daughter's years attending a public *Gymnasium*, she was always an excellent student – always completing her homework on time, writing well in both German and English, eagerly participating in class and behaving flawlessly. Nevertheless, her test scores did not reflect her true intelligence – she just isn't a good test-taker. Sadly, Austrian public schools put far too much weight behind test scores, which only added to her anxiety about taking exams. This is a big reason why she now attends the W@lz School, a private upper-level *Gymnasium* that emphasizes experiential learning, project-based curricula, individual creativity and social competence, instead of just teaching for the test. W@lz doesn't have teachers – only "coaches" and "project leaders." So far, she is thriving there and her overall academic confidence has blossomed. Eventually, she must do her *Matura* exams at an external public school, but I trust that she will be at least as prepared as the "normal" *Gymnasium* pupils.

EXTRACURRICULAR
Learning and After-School
DAY CARE

A 2010 referendum showed that a clear majority (77%) of Viennese believe that all-day schools (*Ganztagsschule* or *offene Schule*) permit a work-family life balance and significantly raise the educational level of the population. This led the Board of Education to allow schools more autonomy to opt for an "open" or all-day schedule integrating instruction with supervised study and leisure time.

Nevertheless, many public schools in Vienna still only offer half-day (morning) instruction, obliging parents to find other forms of after-school day care for younger children.

 wien.gv.at

After-school
DAY CARE
Hort

For pupils attending half-day or part-day schools, public and private after-school day care centers *(Horte)* are available. They serve lunch, provide recreation and extracurricular activities, and help with homework during study time.

Most public primary schools offer after-school day care on site or at a neighboring location.

After-school day care and meals are not offered free of charge but are subsidized for Vienna residents.

REGISTRATION AND PLACEMENT

You can register your child for placement in public after-school day care when you enroll him or her at a school. If a child is already enrolled, you can re-register for the following year in November and December. Registration forms are provided by the school, but can also be submitted online.

 wien.gv.at

If urgent placement is needed (e.g. after changing schools or following a divorce), it is still possible to register during the school year, though availability at your preferred location may be limited.

When you register, you may select up to two preferred locations for your child, though placement in one or the other is not guaranteed. Preference is given to children of working parents. Vienna's Municipal Department for Kindergartens (MA 10) begins to notify parents about placement after the end of the school registration period and no later than May.

Registration for private after- school day care is directly at the respective facility.

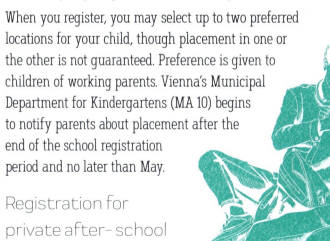

COSTS

Though public schooling is free, day care and meal costs are not (even at all-day schools). Costs (the *Elternbeitrag)* run at €177 per child per month. This covers day care from 11:00 to 17:30 regardless of how many days per week your child attends. Meals cost an additional €68 per month (2019; prices adjusted annually for inflation).

Additional costs for special activities such as day trips, elective courses and event tickets, are not included in the day care costs.

REDUCTION OF DAY CARE COSTS

Reduction of public (or subsidization of private) day care costs is possible for families that meet qualifying income levels and are residents of Vienna. To qualify, your family's monthly net income (including welfare-based income, unemployment benefits, pension, scholarships, stipends, alimony...) must not exceed €2,974.25 per month if you have one child. For each additional child you may subtract €409 per child from your net income, toward the €2,974 cap, i.e. if you have two children and a net income of €3,383 you may subtract €409 for the additional child, leaving you squarely at the €2,974 cap. Applications for the reduction can be submitted to the MA 10 and you must reapply annually.

EXEMPTION FROM MEAL COSTS
FOR PRE-SCHOOL CHILDREN

For qualifying low-income families (total net income less than €1,100 per month), the Vienna Child and Youth Welfare Service (MA 11) covers the meal fees (€68 per month for breakfast, lunch and snacks) for children up to six years of age attending kindergarten, children's groups, or being looked after by child minders. Families with two or more children may subtract €350 per child from their net income, toward the €1,100 cap. A separate application for meal cost exemption must be made for each child. Forms are available at your child's kindergarten or online.

bildung-wien.at

TAX DEDUCTIBILITY OF DAY CARE COSTS

Up to €2,300 in annual care costs for each child up to age 10 is a tax-deductible expense. However, costs related to outside courses, field trips or entry tickets (e.g. for museums and theaters) are not deductible.

Some employers offer an annual tax-free child care "bonus" of up to €500.

NOTE: The figures above were valid at the date of publication. They are adjusted annually for inflation.

TYPES OF EXTRA-CURRICULAR ACTIVITIES

Unlike schools in the United States or United Kingdom, for example, Austrian public schools have no tradition of organized societies, clubs, or sports teams.

However, extracurricular day care at public and private centers offers a mix of learning (homework support) and leisure activities, including sports, informatics, performing arts, creative art, foreign languages and social activities. The offering varies by day care location.

The publicly mandated organization **Bildung im Mittelpunkt organizes study, tutoring and recreational programs for full-day schools, part-day schools and clubs, as well as holiday and summer-school programs, either directly at the school or at study and leisure clubs** *(Lern- und Freizeitklubs)*.

LOCATIONS

bildung-wien.atregistration

DIE KINDERFREUNDE

The largest operator of private kindergartens and day care centers in Vienna also offers study and leisure programs for after-school day care, as well as during holidays and on *Fenstertagen* (days adjacent to official holidays when schools may be closed).

wien.kinderfreunde.at

SPORT CLUBS

Several sport associations in Vienna offer athletic instruction and team sports ranging from American football to yoga. The largest umbrella associations are:

* ASKÖ/WAT Wien (askoewat.wien)
* Sportunion Wien (sportunion-wien.at)

Searchable database of sport associations

MUSIC SCHOOLS

Vienna's public *Musikschulen* offer instruction in instrument playing, singing, composition and dance to children and youths up to 25 years of age. After non-binding registration, the candidate is invited to an informational interview. Admission is subject to availability. Separate registration is required for each location and subject. Prices range from about €70 to €350 per semester, depending on duration and number of participants. Discounts apply for siblings.

WIENXTRA

WienXtra is a city-sponsored agency providing information and multi-faceted after-school programming for children and youths (**wienxtra.at**). If you register for its newsletter, you will also receive the Kinderaktiv card entitling you to some discounts on programs.

WienXtra offers two especially interesting programs for teens and older students:

* **WienXtra Medienzentrum** is a media lab offering advice, tools, software, workshops, free equipment rental, studios and editing suites – all free for teens and older students under 22. Location: Zieglergasse 49/II, 1070 Vienna
medienzentrum.at

* **WienXtra Soundbase** offers musicians between 13 and 26 advice, a recording studio, practice rooms, performance spaces and workshops with professional musicians (check website for specific age restrictions, prices and opening times). Location: Friedrich-Schmidt-Platz 5, 1080 Vienna
soundbase.at

 Listing of other leisure programs for youth

LEARNING DURING the SUMMER holidays

Supervising children over the lengthy summer vacation (July – August) can be a daunting prospect for many working parents. However, many public day care centers offer day care and meals during at least part of the summer for children registered during the school year.

 WienXtra's **Ferienspiel** calendar of events is a must-bookmark for all parents and their information center at the MuseumsQuartier provides information about its (and other private) offerings.

KINDERUNI WIEN

Over two weeks in July, children between 7 and 12 years of age can attend age-appropriate classes in various subject areas, such as science, medicine, technology, agriculture, and economics. Like at a real university, children can select up to two workshops and eight seminars or lectures from a broad catalogue of courses at various academic institutions. Registration begins in mid-May and ends at the beginning of July. Participation is free of charge, demand is high and space is limited.

KINDERUNIKUNST

During the first week of summer vacation, children between six and 14 years of age can choose from a wide array of workshops and seminars covering a spectrum of subjects including architecture, visual art, film, theater, dance, music, and media. Registration begins in mid-May and ends about five weeks later. The program is organized by the University of Applied Arts; participation is free of charge.

KINDER BUSINESS WEEK

Children between eight and 14 years of age can participate in this weeklong program organized by the Chamber of Commerce (WKO) in late July offering interaction with dozens of businesses and enterprises. Children can choose up to 10 events. Lectures last up to 90 minutes and workshops up to five hours. Register online at **kinderbusinessweek.at/**

KINDERFREUNDE SOMMERAKADEMIE

Weeklong day camps (Monday-Friday, 8:00 – 17:00) for children between 6 and 16 years of age throughout the summer months offer a variety of themes such as science, technology, commerce, sport, art, and culture. Weekly costs per child are €220, including transportation, meals and supervision – with a 10% discount for each additional sibling.

MORE SUMMER CAMPS

Filling any gaps are private day care centers, generic summer camps and classes, and other organized leisure activities. Here is a partial listing of some of the larger programs:

Austria.info - Feriencamps in Wien

Feriencamps.at

Berlitz.at

Ferien4kids.at

Ferienwochen.at

SUMMER SCHOOLS

SUMMER CITY CAMPS

These camps at 25 locations throughout Vienna are open to all children attending compulsory schooling (ages 6 to 14) who do not already have a place in a public day care center. Two-week-long remedial courses in German, math and English are offered for pupils in their 5th to 8th school years who have received mid-year grades of "Sufficient" (4) or "Insufficient" (5), as well as "non-regular pupils" who have not been graded. Plentiful leisure activities are offered parallel to the coursework. The courses are tuition-free but cost €50 per child per week for meals (€25 for each additional sibling, free from fourth child on). Registration required (deadline in mid- June).

 Download brochure in English (PDF)

FREE TUTORING AT ADULT EDUCATION CENTERS (*VOLKSHOCHSCHULEN LERNSTATIONEN/VHS*)

For pupils in their 5th to 8th school years, walk-in and cost-free tutoring for math, German and English is available at 18 participating VHS locations during August (Mondays to Thursdays 9:00 to noon). No registration is needed for NMS and AHS pupils.

 Download brochure (PDF, in German)

TUTORING

NACHHILFE

Whether a pupil is failing, just scraping by, wants to improve, or needs to prepare for higher-education entrance exams, there are ample opportunities for coaching and tutoring in Vienna. While after-school day care centers offer pupils general support with their daily homework, they rarely offer intensive tutoring.

Finding the right tutor for your child's needs can be as challenging as finding the right school. Private tutoring institutes vet their freelance tutors, assist you in matching one to your specific needs, and may offer performance guarantees. However, their fees are prohibitive for some. Independent tutors, who can be found on various online platforms, bulletin board postings and through word-of-mouth recommendations, tend to charge less (€15 - €25 per 45-minute session is average), **but choosing the right one can also be challenging.**

CHOOSING A TUTOR

Whether you opt for an institute or a private tutor, here are some questions that will help you make a better choice.

* How long is each session and how much does it cost?
* Where does the tutoring take place?
* What are the tutor's educational and professional qualifications?
* Is there a free (or discounted) trial session?
* How will the institute/tutor evaluate the pupil's needs and make recommendations for tutoring frequency?
* Which teaching methods are employed?
* Are the terms and conditions clear (e.g. registration fees, costs, cancellation, length of contract, refunds, cancellation of a session)?
* Can the institute/tutor provide references?
* Are all learning materials provided by the tutor? Free of charge?
* If tutoring is done at the pupil's home, are tutor's transportation costs included in the price?
* For group tutoring, how many pupils are in a group and by which criteria are the groups formed (ages, ability, subjects etc.)?
* Is it possible to schedule extra sessions on short notice (e.g. before an exam)?
* Is there any performance guarantee (e.g. a refund if grades do not improve)?

Once you select a tutor, be sure to ask him or her to provide some personal identification prior to the first session.

PRIVATE TUTORING
INSTITUTES
NACHHILFEINSTITUTE

Two large institutes in Vienna with tutoring locations across the city are:

LERNQUADRAT
Individual or group training, homework help, intensive courses in all subjects and for all educational levels. Lernquadrat.at (German only)

SCHÜLERHILFE
From €9 per 45-minute session. Money-back guarantee if pupil receives failing mark. Schuelerhilfe.at (German only)

Also offers virtual tutoring via e-learning apps, videos and webinars.

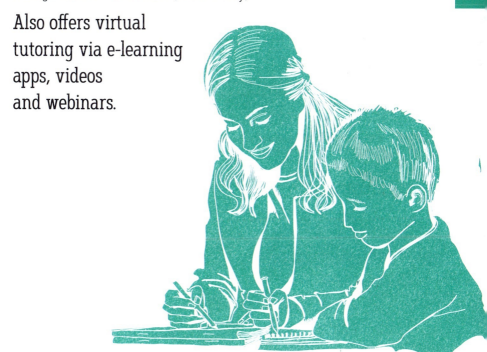

FREELANCE
TUTORS

Independent students and teachers often offer freelance tutoring services and many are listed on online tutoring platforms. Some of these databases help you filter a selection according to price, location, availability, subject and rating, and then connect you directly with the service provider.

BETREUT.AT

Registration, search and e-mail offers from some tutors are free of charge with basic membership. Premium membership gives full access including use of the platform to directly contact tutors and see their references (€35 for one month; €70 for three months; €140 per year). German only.

NACHHILFEN24.AT

Registration and searching for tutors are free, however establishing contact with a freelance tutor is possible only with a premium membership (€20 for one month; €30 for three months; €45 for one year). German only.

WILLHABEN.AT

This general online marketplace shows ads from tutors and does not charge any membership fees for registration or making contact, but it is less easy to filter a selection.

UNIJOBS.AT

Unijobs is an online platform where you can post an advertisement seeking a tutor from the academic community. Posting is free of charge for private individuals.

ADULT-LEARNING CENTERS *VOLKSHOCHSCHULE/VHS*

These facilities offer free weekly courses during the school year for math, German and English, as well as intensive courses during vacations, study coaching, online courses and individual subjects for reasonable prices.

They also offer special courses for non-native German learners "Deutsch Basis & Mehr Kursen" as well as walk-in "Lernstationen" providing free tutoring for math, German and English.

Contact info: +43 1 893 00 83 info@vhs.at

OTHER FREE OR INEXPENSIVE TUTORING

* **Friends Familienzentrum** 2nd district, friends2.at
* **JUHU!** (for disadvantaged children, ages 6-18), 12th district, vereinjuhu.at
* **Kontaktepool Wien** (German-language tutoring for refugee and migrant children), 5th district, stationwien.org/projekte/kontaktepool
* **Lerncafé der Caritas** (for disadvantaged children, ages 6-15) 4th, 10th and 22nd districts, caritas-wien.at
* **WIFI** tutoring for vocational students and apprentices, wifiwien.at
* **Talentify.me** connects pupils and university students with each other for learning together, wifiwien.at/

More **here**

GERMAN INSTRUCTION
FOR NON-NATIVE
PUPILS

WienXtra provides an up-to-date listing of German-language schools and courses for non-native pupils of all ages and levels:

 wienxtra.at

VIENNA LANGUAGE VOUCHERS

For qualifying third country nationals seeking to obtain a residency permit and who have existing family ties in Austria, Vienna provides up to €300 (3x €100) in vouchers for German-language courses (at selected providers) as part of the Start Coaching program. Immigrants to Austria from EU/EEA countries can receive up to €150 in vouchers.

CONTACT THE MUNICIPAL DEPARTMENT FOR INTEGRATION AND DIVERSITY (MA 17) FOR MORE INFO OR TO MAKE AN APPOINTMENT:

* English telephone: 01/90 500 36 – 04

* **startwien.at/en**

TESTIMONIALS

SOPHIE, 48

native Viennese, married to an English native-speaker

My daughter was struggling with her math lessons in *Gymnasium* and neither my expat husband nor I could understand, let alone help her with her studies. Luckily, our neighbor was a retired primary schoolteacher who offered tutoring once a week. Eventually, the level of difficulty was above even her knowledge, so we switched my daughter to a private tutoring institute for intensive preparation for her final exam. It was expensive, but the results were worth it: my daughter was able to rebound from her poor mid-term test results.

NICK*, 38

American expat married to an Austrian

Our kids attended after-school day care at their primary school. It was OK, however, kids are much more "loosely" managed than during school, so stuff can certainly happen. You need to ask your children how things are going on a regular basis and make sure there are no issues. Bullying (or "mobbing" as they call it here) is global. Austria is certainly no exception and, in our case, it happened more often in after-school care than in the classroom.

GEORGE, 52

American expat married to a German, both bilingual

Both of my daughters (age 7 and 10) attended the STEM-based "Engineering For Kids" summer day camp and really loved it. Smaller/local programs can also be found, if you look around. Our kids have also enrolled in a local art and nature camp for the past several years, and the experience has been great. Sports camps are everywhere. Take your pick. Many schools also offer "day camp" during the summer that can come in handy as a fallback.

*name changed.

ADULT EDUCATION

Tertiary
EDUCATION

the basics

THE BOLOGNA PROCESS: BACHELOR/MASTER/ PHD & ECTS POINTS

Since the Bologna Process, a major reform of European higher education, began in 1999, a lot has changed in the Austrian tertiary education sector. The main goal of the reform was to increase the mobility of students and scholars in Europe by introducing a three-tier degree system (bachelor, master, PhD) instead of the two-tier system *(Magister/Diplom-Ingenieur, Doktor)* and by making academic achievements comparable through the European Credit Transfer and Accumulation System (ECTS). In addition, the Bologna reform emphasizes the importance of lifelong learning.

The ECTS ensures that academic performance is recognized, transferable and accumulated transparently across Europe. ECTS points are estimated based on the average workload of a course/lecture. One ECTS point equals about 25 to 30 hours of work. Most types of financial aid and study-based residence permits require students to collect a certain number of ECTS points per year. (Note: ECTS points are unrelated to grades. If you pass a course – no matter whether your final grade is a 1 (Very good) or a 4 (Sufficient) – you get the full number of ECTS points. If you fail the course, you get zero ECTS points). Typically, tertiary education institutions use the Austrian grading scale, which ranges from 1 to 5 (see p 192). If the weighted average of your grades is below 1.5 and your bachelors'/master's thesis was awarded a 1, then congrats to you: you have graduated with distinction (*mit Auszeichnung*)!

Today, the majority of academic degrees offered at Austrian universities follow the Bologna model, so they are either bachelor's degrees (typically six semesters; 180 ECTS), master's degrees (four semesters; 120 ECTS), or PhD programs (typically three years). These new degrees are in the process of replacing the prior system (see table below for examples of some of the changes), but those who originally graduated with a *Magister* or *Diplom-Ingenieur* degree keep the former titles. Today, fewer and fewer departments still award Austrian academic titles, such as the *Magister/Magistra* (usually five years; equivalent to a bachelor plus a master of arts degree), *Diplom-Ingenieur/in* (five years; equivalent to a bachelor plus a master of science degree), or *Doktor* (equivalent to a PhD).

	FORMER ACADEMIC TITLE/DEGREE	TITLE/DEGREE AFTER THE BOLOGNA PROCESS
TITEL	Bakk. (♂ Bakkalaureus, ♀Bakkalaurea)	Bachelor
SPECIALIZATIONS*	bakk. phil., bakk. rer. soc. oec., Bakk. techn., etc.	BSc (Bachelor of Science), BA (Bachelor of Arts), B.Ed. (Bachelor of Education), etc.
EXAMPLE	Sam Sample, Bakk. phil.	Jane Doe, BA
TITEL	Mag. (♂ Magister), Mag.a (♀ Magistra)	Master
SPECIALIZATIONS	Mag. phil., Mag.a rer. soc. oec., Mag. art, etc.	MSc (Master of Science), MA (Master of Arts), M.Ed. (Master of Education), etc.
EXAMPLE	Mag. phil. Samantha Sample	John Doe, MA
TITEL	Dipl.Ing. or DI (♂ Diplom-Ingenieur, ♀ Diplom-Ingenieurin)	Master of Science (MSc)
SPECIALIZATIONS*	Usually awarded for technical degrees	
EXAMPLE	Dipl.Ing. Jane Doe	Jane Doe, MSc
TITEL	Dr. (♂Doktor, ♀ Doktorin)	PhD (Doctor of Philosophy)
SPECIALIZATIONS	Dr. phil., Dr. rer. soc. oec., Dr. techn., etc.	
EXAMPLE	Dr. Sam Sample	John Doe, PhD

* Latin abbreviation indicating the specialization

People who have not passed a higher education entrance exam (such as the Matura) or others who are interested in simply sitting in on lectures can do so within a non-degree program (*außerordentliches Studium*). You can find more information on non-degree programs at the University of Vienna here:

 slw.univie.ac.at

Before we delve into the depths of the Austrian tertiary education system, note that this section focuses on the most common types of university in Vienna. There are, however, other accredited tertiary education institutions in Vienna, such as, for example, the Vienna Music Institute.

Know How to Succeed

WU

EXECUTIVE
ACADEMY

Financial Times
Executive MBA
Ranking:
#45 worldwide

Join the MBA programs of Europe's leading business university:
› real-life content
› students from > 30 nations
› internationally renowned faculty

Global Executive MBA
2 MBA degrees, jointly offered with the University of Minnesota, USA.
3 intern. residencies: Asia, South America, USA.

Professional MBA
Intern. residency: USA. Specialization e.g.
in Finance, Marketing & Sales, Digital Transformation & Data Science,
Energy Management, Project Management, Entrepreneurship & Innovation

WU Executive Academy – Vienna University of Economics and Business
mba@wu.ac.at; executiveacademy.at/mba

INTRICACIES OF THE AUSTRIAN TERTIARY EDUCATION SYSTEM

In Vienna, you can study anything, from astronomy to zoology. If you're still unsure, this online guide presents more information on the degrees offered at Austrian higher education institutions: **studienwahl.at/en**. Beware that in Austria, unlike in the US for example, admission to a specific master's degree usually requires that you hold a bachelor's degree in the same or in a related field.

The two main types of tertiary education institutions are universities (*Universität*) and universities of applied sciences (*Fachhochschule*). The main difference between the two is that universities of applied sciences offer degrees that are rather hands-on and practically oriented. You will find out more about these two types of institutions below.

In contrast to some other countries, Austrian universities emphasize physical attendance and provide distance learning only to a limited degree. There are several different types of courses. Public universities typically differentiate between courses with non-continuous assessment (*nicht-prüfungsimmanente Lehrverantstaltungen,* typically lectures) and courses with continuous assessment (*prüfungsimmanente*

Lehrveranstaltungen, such as seminars or exercises). At the former, attendance is usually voluntary, but as the majority of lectures are not streamed, you should still attend regularly or at least get hold of a colleague's study materials to make sure you can pass the end-of-term exam. In seminars and exercises, attendance is typically mandatory, and you will have to complete assignments and tasks throughout the semester and/or hand in a final paper. At universities of applied sciences, students are usually required to attend most of the courses.

Another surprising fact about Austrian universities is that you can redo exams several times (at public universities up to three times; at universities of applied sciences up to two times).

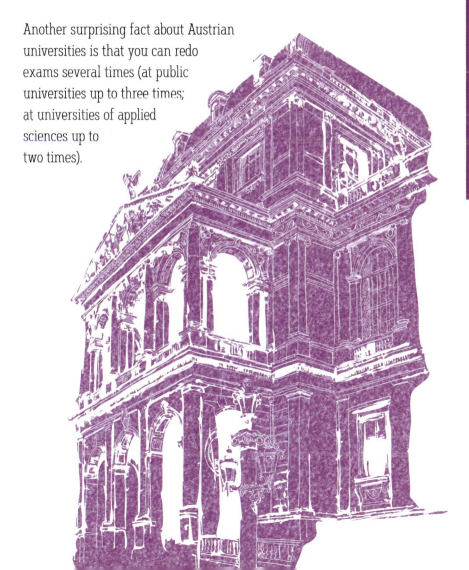

UNIVERSITY RANKINGS

Although the merit of university rankings is debatable, you may be interested in how Austria's universities perform internationally. In the most recent TIMES World University Rankings, the University of Vienna ranked 143, making it the highest-ranked Austrian university. The Vienna University of Technology (Technische Universität Wien or TU Wien) was 251st. The Vienna University of Economics and Business (Wirtschaftsuniversität or WU) also enjoys international prestige – it was ranked 41st in the Financial Times' 2018 comparison of European business schools. It's worth emphasizing that individual faculties, departments or research institutes are often rated higher than the universities as a whole. For example, the University of Vienna's communication sciences and archaeology departments generally perform extremely well on a global scale. Unsurprisingly, Viennese music and arts universities have an excellent international reputation. In the most recent QS

World University Ranking by Subjects, the University of Music and Performing Arts Vienna (see p 208) topped the ranking together with the Juilliard School in New York.

A selection of European schools included in the 2019 TIMES World University Rankings

University of Oxford	1
University of Cambridge	2
Stanford University	3
ETH Zurich	11
LMU Munich	32
University of Amsterdam	62
Sorbonne University	73
University of Vienna	143
Medical University of Vienna	201–250
Vienna University of Technology	251–300

Forms of higher EDUCATION

PUBLIC UNIVERSITY

UNIVERSITÄT / UNI

Vienna has 20 universities whose campuses and buildings are spread across the city. A student population of almost 200,000 makes the Austrian capital the biggest and arguably most vibrant student city in the German-speaking region. Vienna's public and private universities plus their English-taught degrees are listed below.

UNIVERSITY OF VIENNA
UNIVERSITÄT WIEN

With 15 faculties and around 90,000 students, the University of Vienna is the biggest and oldest university in Austria. It offers 178 different degree programs, plus around 40 continuing-education and training programs. The list of English-taught programs can be found here:

 slw.univie.ac.at

VIENNA UNIVERSITY OF ECONOMICS AND BUSINESS
WIRTSCHAFTSUNIVERSITÄT / WU

The Vienna University of Economics and Business has an international focus reflected in its range of degrees taught in English:

* **BSC AND B.BUS:** Business and Economics
* **MSC:** Economics
* **MSC:** Informations systems
* **MSC:** International Management/CEMS
* **MSC:** Marketing
* **MSC:** Quantitative finance
* **MSC:** Socio-ecological economics and policy
* **MSC:** Strategy, innovation and management control
* **MSC:** Supply chain management
* **PHD:** Social and economic sciences, business law, finance, international business taxation, economics and social sciences

In addition, the WU also incorporates the WU Executive Academy, where you can study for an MBA (Master of Business Administration), a Master of Law and other university degrees or certificates. The WU also offers German-language courses.

 wu.ac.at
Course catalog available here.

THE MEDICAL UNIVERSITY OF VIENNA
MEDIZINISCHE UNIVERSITÄT WIEN / MEDUNI

The degrees at the Medical University of Vienna are largely taught in German. They include medicine, dentistry, and medical informatics, plus different PhD programs and post-graduate university courses.

meduniwien.ac.at

VIENNA UNIVERSITY OF TECHNOLOGY
TECHNISCHE UNIVERSITÄT WIEN / TU

The Vienna University of Technology offers degrees in architecture and regional planning, civil engineering, electrical engineering and information technology, informatics, mathematics and geo-information, mechanical engineering and business science, physics, and technical chemistry A number of individual lectures and seminars are taught in English, and you can also take German courses. Here are the TU Wien's English-taught master's degree programs:

* **MSC:** Telecommunications
* **MSC:** Cartography
* **MSC:** DDP Computational logic (Erasmus-Mundus)
* **MSC:** Data science
* **MSC:** Business informatics
* **MSC:** Logic and computation
* **MSC:** Media and human-centered computing

 tuwien.at (English-taught programs are marked "English")

UNIVERSITY **OF NATURAL RESOURCES AND LIFE SCIENCES,** VIENNA

The University of Natural Resources and Life Sciences (Universität für Bodenkultur Wien or BOKU) is a Viennese center for research on renewable resources. You can apply for several master's degree programs in English:

* **MSc:** Biotechnology
* **MSc:** Mountain forestry
* **MSc:** Water management and environmental engineering
* **MSc:** Applied limnology
* **MSc:** Animal breeding and genetics
* **MSc:** Organic agricultural systems

 boku.ac.at

UNIVERSITY **OF VETERINARY MEDICINE,** VIENNA

At the University of Veterinary Medicine, the following degrees are taught in English:

* **MSc:** Comparative biomedicine - Infection biomedicine and tumor signaling pathways
* **MSc:** Comparative vertebrate morphology
* **MSc:** Human-animal interactions
* **MSc:** Evolutionary systems biology

 vetmeduni.ac.at
(English-taught programs are marked with "English")

UNIVERSITY **OF MUSIC AND PERFORMING ARTS**

The Vienna University of Music and Performing Arts (Universität für Musik und Darstellende Kunst Wien or MDW) is one of Europe's most prominent artistic schools. It comprises 24 departments, including the renowned drama school Max Reinhardt Seminar and the Vienna Film Academy. The *mdw* offers German courses.

 mdw.ac.at (this is a list of all study programs; the language of instruction is indicated in the respective curriculum)

UNIVERSITY **OF APPLIED ARTS** **VIENNA**

At the University of Applied Arts Vienna (Universität für Angewandte Kunst Wien), you can study art, architecture, graphic design, industrial design or fashion design. The following degrees are taught in English:

* **MArch:** Architecture
* **MA:** Art & science
* **BA:** Cross-disciplinary strategies
* **MA:** Social design – Arts as urban innovation (taught in German and English)

 dieangewandte.at (this is a list of all study programs; the language of instruction is indicated in the respective curriculum)

ACADEMY **OF FINE ARTS** **VIENNA**

The Academy of Fine Arts Vienna (Akademie der Bildenden Künste Wien) is one of Europe's oldest fine arts schools. It requires German language skills prior to admission or will ask you to learn German during your studies.

More specific information can be found here:

 akbild.ac.at
German-language courses are also offered by the university.

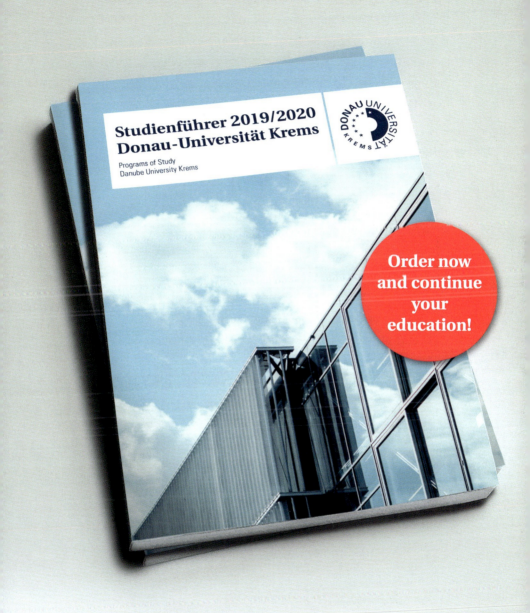

DANUBE UNIVERSITY KREMS

Danube University Krems (Donau-Universität Krems) is a respected university for continuing education in Europe. It is a public university, located around 70km from Vienna in Krems, and offers a range of post-graduate and master's degree courses, for which students pay tuition fees. See a list of the degrees taught in English here:

* **Certified program:** Arbitration and alternative dispute resolution
* **MSc, certified program:** EU regulatory affairs
* **Executive MBA**
* **MA:** Interdisciplinary methods in graphic art, book and document conservation
* **MEng:** Lightweight membrane structures
* **Master** of Administrative Sciences
* **MA:** Media arts cultures
* **Certified program, MA, MA advanced:** Media art histories
* **Certified program:** Migrant entrepreneurship support
* **Doctor of philosophy:** Migration studies
* **MA:** Music management
* **MA,** certified program, expert program: Music for applied media
* **MSc:** Patient blood management
* **Certified program, professional MBA:** Aviation management

Additional modules and certificates are also offered.

 donau-uni.ac.at

PRIVATE UNIVERSITIES

PRIVATUNIVERSITÄTEN

There are also several private universities in Vienna. They are briefly described below, and the English-taught degrees they offer are listed for each institution.

MODUL UNIVERSITY VIENNA

Modul university is specialized in tourism, sustainable development, new media technology and public governance. You can apply for several English-taught BA, MA and PhD programs. Successful completion of an internship of 900 hours is a requirement for graduation. These are the English-taught degree programs:

* **BBA (Bachelor of business administration):** Tourism and hospitality management (three years)
* **BBA:** Tourism, hotel management and operations (four years)
* **BSc:** International management
* **MSc:** Management, international tourism, sustainable development
* **MBA:** Master of business administration
* **PhD:** Doctor of philosophy in business and socioeconomic sciences

 modul.ac.at

WEBSTER UNIVERSITY VIENNA

Webster University Vienna is an American university whose Vienna campus opened in 1981. It is accredited both in the US and in Austria, and the following English-taught degrees are available:

* **BA:** International relations
* **BA:** Management (possible emphasis on international business or marketing)
* **BA:** Media communications
* **BA:** Psychology
* **BSc:** Business administration
* **MA:** International relations, psychology with emphasis on counseling psychology
* **MSc:** Finance, marketing
* **MBA:** Business administration
* **Global Master of Arts (MA):** Earn a degree at five different international campuses

 webster.ac.at

MUSIC AND ARTS
UNIVERSITY OF THE CITY OF VIENNA

At the Music and Arts University of the City of Vienna (Musik und Kunst-Privatuniversität der Stadt Wien or MUK) you can apply for one of 30 BA and MA programs, plus academic diploma programs and preparatory courses. As a prospective student, you need to have advanced proficiency in German, which is the main language of instruction.

 muk.ac.at German is the main language of instruction

SIGMUND FREUD
PRIVATE UNIVERSITY VIENNA

The Sigmund Freud Private University Vienna (Sigmund Freud Privatuniversität Wien) is specialized in psychotherapy and psychology. It offers several degree programs in English.

* **BSc:** Psychology
* **Bakk.pth.:** Psychotherapy science (see academic titles, p 16)
* **Mag.pth.:** Psychotherapy science

 sfu.ac.at

CENTRAL EUROPEAN UNIVERSITY (CEU)

The private university recently relocated from Budapest to Vienna's 10th district because of what it has described as political pressure by the government of Hungary. The university is especially renowned for its social sciences, humanities and business programs and research The language of instruction at the CEU is English.

 ceu.edu

JAM MUSIC LAB PRIVATE UNIVERSITY
FOR JAZZ AND POPULAR MUSIC VIENNA

The Jam Music Lab Private University was founded in 2017. It offers BA and MA degree programs in music and music pedagogy. You need to pass an entrance exam. For some of the programs, the language of instruction is partly English.

 jammusiclab.com (this is a list of all study programs; the language of instruction is indicated in the respective curriculum)

UNIVERSITIES
OF APPLIED SCIENCES
FACHHOCHSCHULEN / FH

Universities of applied sciences (*Fachhochschulen* or *FH*) are institutes of higher education which offer BA and MA programs with an application-oriented focus. (*FHs* are currently not allowed to offer PhD programs, but you can, of course, do a PhD at a university after graduating from an *FH*). There are currently 21 *FHs* in Austria, at which you can study degrees in the following areas: design/art, engineering, social sciences (including for instance communication, journalism, or media management), economics, military/security studies, natural sciences, and health sciences. Most degrees involve one practical training semester, and some are part-time to accommodate working students.

To be admitted, you need some form of general university entrance qualification such as *Matura* (see p 146), *Berufsreifeprüfung* (see p 152) or *Studienberechtigungsprüfung* (see p 250), although some institutions may accept you if you have pertinent professional experience. As the number of students for courses is limited, *FHs* conduct entrance examinations.

Have you come across academic titles such as Mag. FH or Dipl.-Ing. FH? Universities of applied sciences used to award titles with the add-on *FH* for *Fachhochschule*, but today they award the same titles as universities – without the addendum.

These are the five universities of applied sciences in Vienna:

UNIVERSITY OF APPLIED SCIENCES BFI VIENNA
FOCUSES: finance, sales, project management, media, business

UNIVERSITY OF APPLIED SCIENCES, FH CAMPUS WIEN COMPETITIVE IN PHYSIOTHERAPY AND OTHER HEALTH SCIENCES
FOCUSES: architecture/building, bioengineering, engineering, administration and management, health sciences, social sciences

UNIVERSITY OF APPLIED SCIENCES TECHNIKUM WIEN
FOCUSES: electronics, computer science, human factors and sports, engineering

FH WIEN UNIVERSITY OF APPLIED SCIENCES OF THE WKW
FOCUSES: business, corporate communication, human resources, marketing, real estate, finance, journalism, content production and digital media management, tourism

LAUDER BUSINESS SCHOOL
FOCUSES: business administration, management and leadership, finance, business analytics

FERDINAND PORSCHE FERN FH (LOWER AUSTRIA)
Distance learning

FOCUSES: aging services management, business administration, business psychology, information systems

These universities of applied sciences can be easily reached from Vienna:

UNIVERSITY OF APPLIED SCIENCES KREMS
FOCUSES: applied chemistry, business administration, digital business transformation and innovation, export-oriented management, informatics, international wine business, marketing, tourism, biotechnology

UNIVERSITY OF APPLIED SCIENCES WIENER NEUSTADT
FOCUSES: sport, security, health, engineering, business

UNIVERSITY OF APPLIED SCIENCES ST. PÖLTEN
COMPETITIVE IN PHYSIOTHERAPY
AND OTHER HEALTH SCIENCES
FOCUSES: media and economics, media and digital technologies, informatics and security, mobility, health, social sciences

UNIVERSITY OF APPLIED SCIENCES BURGENLAND
COMPETITIVE IN PHYSIOTHERAPY AND
OTHER HEALTH SCIENCES
FOCUSES: business studies with focus on Central and Eastern Europe, information technology and information management, social work, energy and environmental management, health

You can find a complete list of Austrian universities of applied sciences here: **oesterreich.gv.at**

UNIVERSITY COLLEGES OF
TEACHER EDUCATION

The university colleges of teacher education *(Pädagogische Hochschulen)* train primary schoolteachers in cooperation with universities. Prospective students need to have a *Matura* (or equivalent) and in addition they must pass a degree course aptitude test. The bachelor's degree takes at least four years, and students receive a teaching certificate upon completion. After completing the BA, you can continue with a master's degree (1-1.5 years).

FINDING A PLACE

ADMISSION REQUIREMENTS AND PROCESS

ADMISSION AT TERTIARY EDUCATION INSTITUTIONS: THE BASICS

Admission requirements, procedures and deadlines differ between individual institutions. Make sure to contact the institution you want to apply to as soon as possible to inquire about the admission process. Beware that some degrees, especially those with entrance tests, require you to pre-register online.

THE TYPICAL ADMISSION PROCESS INCLUDES THE FOLLOWING STEPS:

* Online pre-registration (if required)
* Submission of all required documents, including proof of higher education entrance examination (see International Academic Recognition and Nostrification, p 224) and proof of German language skills
* If applicable: entrance exam, interview or audition, or handing in your portfolio (often required at art schools)
* If you're accepted, you receive an approval notification *(positiver Zulassungsbescheid)*
* With this approval notification, you can apply for a confirmation of registration *(Aufenthaltsbescheinigung), visa (Visum)* or residence permit*(Aufenthalts-bewilligung);* (see Study-Related Visa and Residence Permits, p 219).
* Note that if you move into an apartment/housing in Austria, you are required to register with the local registration office *(Meldebehörde)* within three days of moving in
* For enrollment *(Immatrikulation),* you must submit your approval notification, a copy of your passport/proof of citizenship, all required forms, and a passport photo.

Documents may have to be translated and/or notarized. Note that entrance exams – if your selected field of study has them – are mandatory for all applicants, even if you've passed comparable tests in your home country. Also, once you're admitted, you may be required to take additional exams (e.g. a Latin exam if you study medicine), so inquire in advance with the respective office if this is the case for you. Usually, you need to pass these exams prior to reaching a particular stage of your study.

The following two sections provide more information on the admission process at the University of Vienna and at universities of applied sciences. To learn more about admission to other tertiary education institutions, check out **aufnahmepruefung.at**, which has useful insights and students' personal experiences with entrance procedures at Austrian tertiary education institutions.

ADMISSION TO THE UNIVERSITY OF VIENNA

Contact Teaching Affairs and Student Services with plenty of time to spare (**slw.univie.ac.at/en**), to ensure you have all your documents in order. It takes at least 12 weeks until international applications are processed, which frequently interferes with visa applications. The university recommends that students who fulfill language requirements should apply by July 15 at the latest. Admission to bachelor and diploma programs requires students to provide evidence of C1-level German language skills. Beware, the University of Vienna does not cooperate with agencies offering to process students' applications and does not have any cooperation agreements (except for exchange programs such as Erasmus+). If you are interested in studying at the University of Vienna, you have to personally apply for admission. Here are some FAQ's from international applicants:

 blog.univie.ac.at

ADMISSION TO THE UNIVERSITIES OF APPLIED SCIENCES

As the number of students per course is typically limited, universities of applied sciences select students through admission tests and interviews. For extra-occupational studies, applicants with relevant professional experience may be preferred or even accepted without higher education entrance qualifications (see p 223). Deadlines vary between different universities of applied sciences, so make sure you get the information you need soon enough!

UNIVERSITY PREPARATION PROGRAMS

Once you have been admitted to an Austrian university but need to pass additional examinations, you may benefit from university preparation programs. Their purpose is to prepare non-Austrian students for supplementary exams through intensive courses in German as a foreign language, English, math, physics, chemistry, biology, history and geography. You can find more information here:

 oead.at

STUDY-RELATED VISA AND RESIDENCE PERMITS

CITIZENS OF THE EUROPEAN ECONOMIC AREA (EEA) AND SWISS NATIONALS

As a national of an EEA country or a Swiss citizen, you need only your passport – not a visa – to stay in Austria for up to three months. If you meet certain requirements, you can remain longer. In this event, you need to get a confirmation of registration (*Anmeldebescheinigung*) from the competent residence authority (embassy, consulate general). The prerequisites for this are that the main purpose of your stay is your training/education (you have confirmation of admission from a higher education institution), and that you have health insurance and sufficient means of subsistence (the amount depends on the individual case). Forms of proof of sufficient financial resources can include a savings book from an Austrian bank, a bank account in your country of origin, or a declaration of liability signed by someone living in Austria

THIRD-COUNTRY NATIONALS STAYING FOR UP TO SIX MONTHS

As a third-country national, you need a visa C (for stays up to 90 days) or a visa D (for stays between 90 to 180 days) to study in Austria. (Certain countries, such as Australia and Peru, are exempted from this visa requirement. You can find more information on visa exemptions here:

 bmi.gv.at

THESE DOCUMENTS ARE REQUIRED FOR APPLICATION AT THE COMPETENT AUSTRIAN REPRESENTATIVE AUTHORITY (EMBASSY, CONSULATE GENERAL):

* Completed application form
* Valid travel document (validity period must exceed the validity period of the visa by at least three months; must include at least two empty pages and have been issued within 10 years)
* Passport-size photograph following ICAO criteria (see **icao.int/Security**)
* Proof of health insurance for whole duration of stay in Austria
* Proof of sufficient financial means (rates adjusted each year, but usually around €500-€900 per month depending on your age)
* Proof of tuition fee payment at Austrian higher education institution

Frustratingly, Austria does not allow in-country visa extensions, so if your visa has expired you need to leave the country and apply for a new one. Visa applications are usually handled by the Austrian Embassy in your country of residence.

Careful: The visas C and D do not allow you to be gainfully employed or self-employed. If you plan to work during your studies, check out the information on p 232.

THIRD-COUNTRY NATIONALS STAYING FOR MORE THAN SIX MONTHS

If you want to stay in Austria longer than six months, you need a student residence permit – a small card that also serves as your ID, and which is issued for 12 months. You can apply for this residence permit at the relevant Austrian representative authority (in Vienna, this is MA 35 Einwanderung und Staatsbürgerschaft, **wien.gv.at/kontakte/ma35**) - or abroad, by submitting the following documents:

* Completed application form
* Photocopy of valid travel document
* Birth certificate or equivalent document
* Recent passport-size photograph following ICAO criteria (see **icao.int/Security**)
* Police clearance certificate
* Notification of admission to Austrian education institution
* Proof of sufficient financial means for your stay (rates are adjusted each year, but they are usually around €500-€900 per month depending on your age)
* Proof of accommodation in Austria (e.g. reservation at student hall, rental contract)
* Proof of (travel) health insurance (amount of coverage at least €30,000)

If the degree program you're applying for has an entrance exam, then the university can issue a "conditional notification of admission" with which you can apply for the student residence permit.

Make sure to apply for the renewal of your residence permit in time (at the earliest three months before it expires). You can find more information on deadlines, forms, etc. here:

wien.gv.at

oead.at

RED-WHITE-RED CARD
ROT-WEISS-ROT-KARTE

Once you have graduated from a master's degree or the second stage of a diploma degree at an Austrian tertiary education institution, you can apply for another type of residence title, the Red-White-Red Card. For this, you need to fulfil certain requirements, which you can find here:

 migration.gv.at

ENTRANCE PROCEDURES: EXAMS, INTERVIEWS, PORTFOLIOS, AUDITIONS & THE STEOP

The following tertiary education institutions generally require students to pass an entrance exam and/or a personal interview: universities of applied sciences and university colleges of teacher education.

At most art schools, you need to hand in a portfolio or similar proof of your eligibility. Music and drama schools usually require applicants to pass auditions.

At public universities, the admission requirements differ between fields of study. At the University of Vienna, most bachelor, teacher accreditation and diploma studies have an entrance exam in the summer or fall before the term begins and/or a so-called introductory and orientation period (*Studien-eingangs- und Orientierungsphase* or STEOP), in the first semester. Only students who pass all STEOP exams (they comprise 8-20 ETCS points), can continue with their studies. Students can re-sit these exams three times.

If you plan on attending a private university, inquire with the respective institution to learn about their admission procedures.

International academic recognition and nostrification

Nostrification (*Nostrifizierung*) refers to the recognition/ approbation by a particular higher education institution of degrees acquired abroad. Be prepared to submit (at least) the following documents:

* Copy of passport
* Proof of the status of the institution where the degree was acquired
* Detailed documents describing the degree (e.g. study plan, transcript of records, term papers, certificates, etc.)
* Certificate confirming graduation and the award of the academic degree
* Information about the envisaged professional occupation of the applicant

Documents are usually handed in as originals or notarized transcripts, and if they are in any other language than German or English, notarized translations are also required.

The National Academic Recognition Center (Nationales Informationszentrum für akademische Anerkennung), or ENIC Austria, is Austria's information center regarding the approbation of academic degrees. It is the Austrian leg of the international European Network of Information Centers (ENIC). For a fee of €150 for up to two qualifications and €200 for three or more, you can submit your documents online (**aais.at**) and have them assessed.

For more information on the approbation of qualifications acquired abroad, consult the advisory center for migrants (AST Perspektive – Beratungszentrum für Migranten und Migrantinnen).

COSTS

TUITION FEES

Non-Austrians are often surprised that tertiary education is largely free (or extremely cheap). If you have to pay tuition fees, you usually pay them online in advance for each term.

If you want to study at the University of Vienna and are a citizen of the EU or the EEA or are a Swiss citizen, you pay a €20.20 membership fee per month for the Student Association (Österreichische Hochschülerschaft or ÖH). Only if it takes you longer than eight semesters to finish your bachelor's degree or longer than six semesters to finish your master's degree do you have to pay €383.56 per term.

As a general rule, students who are not citizens of the countries mentioned above pay a tuition fee of €726.72 per term plus the €20.20 membership fee for the ÖH. However, the fee can differ depending on your country of origin.

At universities of applied sciences, EU/EEA students usually pay €363.36 per semester plus the ÖH membership fee.

As is to be expected, tuition fees are much higher at private universities. Inquire with the respective institution.

GRANTS AND FINANCIAL AID

Different types of financial support are available to students in Austria. The Study Grant Authority (Stipendienstelle) is responsible for information, applications, appeals and interventions regarding study grants, study allowances, transport cost allowances, grants upon completion of studies, insurance cost subsidies, mobility grants, and grants for studies abroad.

The bad news is that if you are a non-Austrian citizen, you must fulfill special conditions to be granted equal status with Austrian citizens regarding all kinds of direct federal aid for students. The rules say that EEA citizens are equal with Austrians if they or one of their parents are migrant workers (*Wanderarbeiter*) or if they are "sufficiently integrated." Third-country nationals need permanent residence status, and refugees need proof of their refugee status to be considered. Unfortunately, the detailed legal parameters are so complex that non-Austrian citizens are well-advised to contact the responsible study grant department for further information.

A great overview of all grants and scholarships is provided here: **grants.at/en** and here **stipendium.at/english-information**.

STUDY
abroad

Austrian tertiary education institutions increasingly encourage the internationalization of studies and student mobility. Some degrees (at public and private universities or at universities of applied sciences) require students to spend at least one term abroad, and the possibility of a voluntary internship/exchange or research stay in another country is open to all students.

The central authority for international mobility is the Austrian Academic Exchange Service (Österreichischer Austauschdienst or OeAD). They cooperate with exchange programs such as Erasmus (organizes exchanges within Europe for schools, vocational education, tertiary education, and adult education), Joint Study (bilateral contracts between a Viennese university and a partner university mostly in non-European countries), or CEEPUS (Central European Exchange Program for University Studies, organizes exchanges with universities in Bulgaria, Croatia, Hungary, Poland, Slovakia and Slovenia, amongst others.). If you are enrolled in an Austrian tertiary education institution and want to study abroad, get in contact with your school's international exchange coordinator. You can also find more information on exchange programs here:

 oead.at/en

Other organizational MATTERS

SCHOOL YEAR

At public universities, the first winter semester (*Wintersemester*) is typically from October to January, and the summer semester (*Sommersemster*) lasts from March to June. This means that the summer break spans July, August and September, and the term break comprises February. Term dates may differ at universities of applied sciences and private universities.

HOUSING

Students in Vienna can apply for student housing (there are several organizations, such as home4students). You can find more information on student housing in our SURVIVIAL GUIDE FOR HOUSING.

INSURANCE

If you are a student and do not yet have health insurance (for instance through a family member or a job), you can register for voluntary self-insurance at very reasonable rates (around €60 per month). Check here whether you meet the prerequisites:

 sozialversicherung.at

GERMAN COURSES **FOR UNIVERSITY STUDENTS** AND ADULTS

Although the number of courses and degrees taught in English is rising, you will likely run into challenges if you do not speak German. Many universities offer German courses at different proficiency levels, sometimes for free or for very little money, so check whether this is the case first. There are also numerous private institutes where you can learn German.

HERE IS A LIST OF INSTITUTIONS OFFERING GERMAN COURSES FOR UNIVERSITY STUDENTS AND ADULTS:

* **ACTILINGUA ACADEMY:** German courses, summer school and holiday courses (12-19 years)

* **ADVENTUM INSTITUT:** German courses (14+ years)

* **ALINGUA CONCORDIS:** German courses (16+ years)

* **ALPHA SPRACHINSTITUT AUSTRIA:** German courses (16+ years)

* **BERLITZ:** German courses for young people and adults

* **BFI – BERUFSFÖRDERUNGSINSTITUT:** German courses for adults

* **DAS SPRACHENSTUDIO:** German courses (16+ years)

* **DEUTSCH AKADEMIE:** German courses (16+ years), summer courses (16+ years)

* **DEUTSCHINSTITUT:** German courses (16+ years), summer courses (16+ years)

* **DEUTSCHOTHEK SPRACHSCHULE:** German courses (16+ years), summer courses (16+ years)

* **DIALOG** – Der Sprachcampus: German courses (16+ years)

- **ELOQUENT SPRACHINSTITUT:** German courses (15+ years)
- **IFU SPRACHENSCHULUNG:** German courses for adults
- **INNES VIENNA:** German courses (16+ years), summer and winter school (16+ years)
- **INTERNATIONALES KULTURINSTITUT (IKI):** German courses (16+ years), summer courses (16+ years)
- **LEARN QUICK:** German courses for adults
- **LOQUI SPRACH- UND BILDUNGSINSTITUT:** German courses (16+ years)
- **MERIDIAN SPRACHZENTRUM:** German courses (16+ years)
- **ÖJAP – ÖSTERREICHISCHE JUNGARBEITERINNENBEWEGUNG:** German courses (16+ years)
- **ÖSTERREICHISCHE ORIENT-GESELLSCHAFT:** German courses (16+ years)
- **SPRACHENZENTRUM DER UNIVERSITÄT WIEN:** German courses (16+), summer intensive courses (16+ years)
- **VHS –** Wiener Volkshochschulen: German courses (15+ years)
- **VORSTUDIENLEHRGANG:** German courses preparing international students for supplementary examinations
- **WIFI –** Wirtschaftsförderungsinstitut: German courses for adults

If you meet specific requirements, the City of Vienna will subsidize your German language courses with a Vienna language voucher *(Wiener Sprachgutschein)* of up to €300. You can get the voucher together with the Vienna Education Booklet (*Wiener Bildungspass*) and can use it with one of the official course providers here:

 wien.gv.at

(The Vienna Education Booklet is a guide funded by the City of Vienna informing non-Austrians about employment and education. You find more information here:

 startwien.at

WORKING DURING YOUR STUDIES

Do you need or want to earn money while you're studying?

If you are from the EEA or a Swiss national, you have free access to the Austrian labor market and do not need special approval to work (*Arbeitnehmerfreizügigkeit*).

If you are a third-country national here on a visa C or D and you want to work during your studies, you need to apply for a visa "for gainful employment." Note that there are possible restrictions on how many hours you can work per week, and that even unpaid work, like unpaid traineeships or internships, can fall into this category.

If you are a third-country national and you are in Austria with a residence permit, then you need a work permit, for which your employer has to apply. With the work permit, you can work up to 20 hours per week.

LEGAL ADVICE, COUNSELLING AND COACHING

The Austrian bureaucratic and legal system is infamously complicated, and so you will likely need additional support to deal with all the bureaucratic hurdles. Luckily, several service points offer legal support and career advice but also psychological help, usually free of charge.

The Austrian National Union of Students (Österreichische Hochschüler_innenschaft or ÖH) is the official political and legal representative of all students vis-a-vis ministries. The members of the ÖH are elected every two years. The different ÖH service points offer information on study-related questions through its website, via email (**oeh@oeh.ac.at**) and in personal appointments. The office for foreign students helps with problems related to visas, studies, German proficiency, tuition fees and financial aid etc. It offers legal counsel via email (**ar@oeh.ac.at**) in English, Turkish and Spanish.

As an international student you face a few additional challenges: a language barrier, an unfamiliar academic environment, and possibly homesickness. Six psychological counseling service locations support students and prospective students with questions related to your choice of study, personal development and concerns, and mental health issues. These services (advice, coaching, supervision, counseling) are free of charge and can be accessed online (also anonymously) and in person.

Many Austrian tertiary education institutions also have career guidance centers that offer information on your choice of profession.

Extracurricular
ACTIVITIES
during tertiary
education

INTRO

NO SOCIETY & CLUB TRADITION, BUT MANY ALTERNATIVES

Austrian universities do not have a society-and-club tradition like the US or the UK, nor does anything remotely comparable to the American university sports system exist here. However, if you want to do something creative, practice sports or get involved in politics, there are plenty of opportunities to choose from.

SPORTS

The University Sports Institute (Universitäts-sportinstitut or USI) is part of the University of Vienna and offers around 120 types of sports courses for very affordable prices to students and former students. You can find anything from aerial bungee training (€64-€108 per semester), indoor skydiving (€165-€185 per semester), jazz or Bollywood dance (€57-€96 per semester) to yoga (€64-€129 per semester), football (€15-€29 per semester), swimming (€16-€33 per semester) and various workouts (around €20-€40 per semester). You can also acquire professional certificates, for instance as a masseur. The instructors are fully qualified professionals. Check out the program online and register as soon as the registration period starts in the fall, as some courses are very popular.

In addition, there are numerous private sports clubs (*Sportvereine*). A complete list of all Viennese sports clubs can be found here:

wien.gv.at
Usually, you pay a small yearly fee.

The Austrian Sports Federation for the Disabled (Österreichischer Behindertensportverband or ÖBSV) is not affiliated with the university and offers courses for people with disabilities.

Of course, you can also join private gyms, but be careful not to get unknowingly wrapped up in minimum-duration contracts.

CREATIVE ACTIVITIES: MUSIC, WRITING ETC.

Some departments (e.g. at the University of Vienna or Webster University) have podcasts and radio programs as well as writing, acting or other creative societies, which are often run by students.

If you're musically inclined, you could join the Vienna University Philharmonic which consists of two orchestras and eight choirs in which more than 1,000 musicians and singers of different musical levels and age groups perform regularly. The repertoire includes classical music, pop, world music, musicals, and jazz.

Of course, there are also many private organizations and clubs in Vienna where amateurs can learn to sing, act, or perform.

POLITICS

You also have the option of being politically active by joining the Austrian Students' Union (Österreichische Hochschüler_innenschaft or ÖH): **oeh.ac.at/en/about-us/join**. Elections are held every two years in the spring.

INTERNSHIPS

Some degrees require students to complete internships (especially *Fachhochschulen* and private universities, but also a few departments at the University of Vienna). Students can find internship opportunities themselves in the private sector. Tertiary education institutions typically advertise open positions for tutors, research and project assistants and study assistants.

Tips for (prospective) STUDENTS

You have just moved to Vienna to study here?

The psychological counseling services have the following advice for you:

* Ask questions – in or outside of class, via email and by consulting support services (such as the Student Service Center of your department, the ÖH, or the psychological counseling services).

* Inquire about free tutorials. Many departments offer support for essay writing and academic research.

* Find other international and local students who have spent time abroad and ask them what has facilitated their acclimatization.

* Participate in extracurricular activities (see p 134): it's a great way to make friends and acquire new skills.

Transition: POST-GRADUATE EDUCATION, adult education

Congrats, you have graduated! What's next? If you want to immediately continue your academic education, you will be happy to hear that most tertiary education institutions offer MA and PhD programs for little money. If you're lucky you may even get a paid PhD position that involves research, teaching and administrative tasks. Of course, there are countless other options for further academic or professional training, whether you want to catch up on scholastic qualifications, learn a new skill, or go back to university as a senior student. Learn more about second-chance and adult education in the next section!

TESTIMONIALS

FAISAL, 29
mechanical engineer

After completing a degree in mechanical engineering and working for four years in Pakistan, I moved to Austria in 2016 to pursue my passion: getting an MSc in aerospace engineering. Good English-taught courses in this field are rare, and so – also in view of the quality of education and the prospects after graduation – the Fachhochschule Wiener Neustadt was the ideal choice (I graduated in March 2019).

The process of getting all the paperwork for the student visa verified by the embassy's legal counsel and legalized is lengthy and demanding. This first step alone can take three to six months. Only then can you apply for the student residence permit, which again takes between two and eight months. All in all, be prepared to invest energy, funds and patience during this phase.

What I like about Austrian universities of applied sciences and technical universities is that there are niche topics and specialized research groups. However, the opportunities for students to get involved in industry projects are scarce, mostly because the employment laws make it hard for companies to offer internships or collaborations for thesis projects. Also, keep in mind that while Austria has several brilliant companies, few of them are really global or multinational. If you're coming here seeking professional opportunities, then do your research first. Overall, life in Vienna was initially quite adventurous for me, but I survived the transition period with little German skills. Still, my advice to all expats is to learn as much German as possible before your arrival, and don't stop once you are here.

KEVIN, 29
university lecturer & researcher

I moved to Austria in late 2017, and arrived with the ambitious goal of learning German. In the time since, I've enrolled in five different German-language courses (plus one-on-one tutoring) at three different institutions. And to answer your next question: no, I'm nowhere near fluent. Throughout this process, I learned that when it comes to German-language courses, you get what you pay for. While my first course (A1 level) was also the cheapest one, it's still the case that, the higher you go in the levels, the harder it is to find quality active teaching (much less at a place that doesn't cost an arm and a leg). If you settle for the cheaper courses, be prepared to have teachers who make very clear that they'd rather be anywhere else than in that classroom. I've also discovered that a few places, like DeutschAkademie, have their own system for enrolling and assessing your speaking level, which often means that simply having a certificate won't be enough to enroll. Looking back, I should've probably accepted that one-on-one tutoring was what I needed, despite it being the most expensive option. Again: You get what you pay for.

KEVIN, 29

university lecturer & researcher

Coming from the American university system, I learned a few things about credentials and how they carry over into the Austrian system. For one thing, the term "associate's degree" doesn't quite translate here (except maybe at Webster – which is an American university) – although you can maybe find an equivalent when you're talking about vocational (*Berufsausbildung*) training. As for my bachelor's degree, it was important to some of my employers and colleagues that I clarify what we mean by "GPA," what "standardized tests" are, and what "Gen. Eds." are. Moreover, there seems to be a lot of social capital given to credentials here. My office door says my name, followed by BA MA, although in the US you wouldn't necessarily list degrees below a PhD. Don't be alarmed when you see your degrees listed on letter envelopes or name tags.

MATTHEW, 37

self-employed language trainer

When I started my education at university in Vienna, I found myself in a situation straight from a Franz Kafka novel. My certificates were not accepted in Austria, so I found myself waiting in long lines to find out how I could proceed. The bureaucrat in the admissions office sat with his feet on the desk, refusing to acknowledge the presence of another human in the room except to bark that nobody is allowed to accompany applicants. I was informed that I would have to take an English course. I replied that we speak English in Australia. He grunted and sent me off to a geography and history course that took a year before I could start university. What I soon noticed was that the way of politeness in the Anglo-Saxon world – being meek, kind and self-deprecating – is seen as weakness in Vienna. Shouting seems to spur politeness. And a title helps as well. Once inside the system I had nothing to complain about. I found the classes informative and felt that the pursuit of knowledge was still treasured over mere job training. The professors were fantastic and inspired me to continue to the PhD level. Naturally, being a free university made it that we could not enjoy the bells and whistles a university in the English-speaking world does, but I was not bothered at all. I was, after all, there to learn, and I recommend the free or near-free education available through university to everybody who can attend.

Second-chance AND ADULT education

the basics

Life-long learning – the idea that people of all ages should have access to education and training – is one of the central pillars of modern educational policy. Adult education is now one of the largest education sectors in Austria, and especially in Vienna you can benefit from a wide range of courses, trainings and programs, sometimes for very low fees.

FORMS OF SECOND-CHANCE/
ADULT EDUCATION

Here, we differentiate between second-chance education *(Zweiter Bildungsweg)* and adult education (*Erwachsenenbildung*). By second-chance education, we mean catching up on educational qualifications, such as preparatory courses for the higher education entrance examination. Adult education comprises all other types of personal and career advancement programs available to adults. Second-chance and adult education are provided by private academies and institutions (such as the *Volkshochschulen*, WIFI and BIFI), public and private universities and universities of applied sciences, as well as the Public Employment Service (AMS), and general public libraries.

YOU CAN FIND MORE DETAILED INFORMATION HERE:

* **erwachsenenbildung.at**

* **oe-cert.at**

* AST Perspektive – Beratungszentrum für Migranten und Migrantinnen

* Wiener ArbeitnehmerInnen Förderungsfonds

metropole.city

FINANCIAL
MATTERS

Several types of financial aid are available for people who want to continue their education. For instance, you can apply for a €300-€3,000 training account (*Bildungskonto*) at the Wiener ArbeitnehmerInnen Förderungsfond (WAFF). Find more information about the training account here: **waff.at/foerderungen/bildungskonto**.

If you are employed in Austria, you can also apply for educational leave (*Bildungskarenz*) of up to one year in total (to be completed within four years). During this time, as long as you attend a training course for at least 20 hours per week, you are entitled to financial support in the amount of unemployment benefit. For more information, contact the Public Employment Service Austria (see AMS, p 252).

If you are a member of the Viennese Chamber of Labor (Arbeiterkammer or AK Wien), you may be eligible for the AK educational voucher (AK Bildungsgutschein) of €270.

Second-chance EDUCATION

Zweiter Bildungsweg

The purpose of second-chance education (*zweiter Bildungsweg*) is to catch up on educational qualifications, from acquiring a lower secondary school completion certificate (*Pflichtschulabschluss*), to passing a higher education entrance exam.

LOWER SECONDARY
SCHOOL COMPLETION
CERTIFICATE
PFLICHTSCHULABSCHLUSS

You sit exams in six areas of competence (German, English, mathematics, career orientation and two elective subjects such as creativity and design, health and social care,

nature and technology, or an additional language). Free preparatory courses are on offer for instance by *Volkshochschulen* and *Berufsförderungs-institute.*

ALTERNATIVE WAYS TO GAIN ACCESS TO HIGHER EDUCATION

In case you do not have a *Matura* or *Matura*-equivalent, there are several ways of gaining access to tertiary education.

Higher education entrance examination for external students *(Externistenreifeprüfung)*

If you have been home-schooled or educated at a non-accredited school, you can do the higher education entrance examination for external students (*Externistenreifeprüfung*). Requirements are the completion of eight years of education and an application for admission submitted to the appropriate Regional Education Board (Landesschulrat or Stadtschulrat in Vienna). Preparatory courses are offered at adult education institutions.

Limited education entrance examination
(Studienberechtigungsprüfung)

If you already know exactly what you want to study, you can opt for the limited higher education entrance examination (*Studienberechtigungsprüfung* or *SBP*). You take the *SBP* with the aim of applying for one specific course of study, which means that a later change of study program is difficult or impossible. The requirements are:

* For studies at universities, universities of applied sciences and colleges for teacher education, you need to be at least 20 years old; for studies at colleges (see *Kolleg*, p 141) you need to be at least 22 years old.

* You need to either be a citizen of the EEA, or have had your main residence in Austria for the last five consecutive years, or have refugee status, be entitled to be granted asylum or have subsidiary protection status

* You must have some form of relevant experience in the field you are applying for.

The *SBP* consists of five individual exams: writing an essay; tests in two to three mandatory subjects that depend on the study field you seek to enter and tests in one to two elective subjects (topics related to the envisaged study degree).

General higher education entrance examination for leavers of apprenticeship training and vet schools (*Berufsreifeprüfung*)

If you have initial vocational education (apprenticeship qualification, medium-level secondary, technical and vocational qualifications etc.) and you want to either move up into a higher salary grade or go to university, you can sit a general higher education entrance examination (see *Berufsreifeprüfung*, p 152).

Adult
EDUCATION
Erwachsenenbildung

INSTITUTIONS THAT OFFER ADULT EDUCATION PROGRAMS

A number of institutions in Vienna offer adult education programs, including:

* Institute for Economic Promotion (Wirtschaftsförderungsinstitut or WIFI)
* Austrian Public Employment Service (Arbeitsmarktservice Österreich or AMS) (see p 252)
* Vocational Training Institute (Berufsförderungsinstitut or BFI)
* *Volkshochschule*
* Federal Institute for Adult Education (Bundesinstitut für Erwachsenenbildung or bifeb)
* Erasmus+ Adult Education

PUBLIC EMPLOYMENT SERVICE AUSTRIA

The Public Employment Service Austria (Arbeitsmarktservice or AMS) is the country's leading provider of labor-market related services, and also offers qualification opportunities and financial assistance. The AMS has career information centers (*BerufsInfoZentrum* or *BIZ*) for consultation about various professions and employment opportunities. It also offers training to unemployed people, employed jobseekers, first-time workers, and school-leavers.

VOLKSHOCHSCHULEN

At Viennese *Volkshochschulen*, you can prepare for catching up on s cholastic qualifications, but you can also acquire skills in the following areas: languages; health and sports; arts and crafts; computers and multimedia; economics and management; personal development; science; politics and society; pedagogy; technology. The language of instruction is typically German.

CONTINUING EDUCATION COURSES

Many tertiary education institutions offer continuing education courses (*Universitätslehrgänge* or *Weiterbildungslehrgänge*). In these courses, you can deepen or acquire supplementary qualifications in a specific subject area. It is often a requirement to have completed a relevant course of study or to possess relevant professional experience.

The University of Vienna, for example, offers continuing education courses in the areas of education and social work, health and natural sciences, international affairs and economics, communication and media, and law.

At the Executive Academy, which is part of the Wirtschaftsuniversität Wien, you can complete part-time courses in marketing and sales, tourism and event management, or health care management.

VOCATIONAL SCHOOLS FOR ADULTS AND POST-SECONDARY VOCATIONAL COURSES

There are also various opportunities to catch up on vocational training and academic qualifications, such as the Berufsförderungsinstitut (BFI) or the Wirtschaftsförderungsinstitut (WIFI). At these vocational education training (VET) schools for adults you can acquire educational qualifications, including passing the higher education entrance examination, with evening courses. You can also attend more advanced post-secondary VET courses in: structural engineering; chemistry and chemical engineering; computer science and IT; media technology and media management; tourism; economic professions etc.

MASTER OF BUSINESS ADMINISTRATION (MBA) AND MASTER OF LAWS (LL.M.)

Numerous Viennese institutions offer Masters of Business Administration (MBA). Here's a list of all such programs:

 mba-vergleich.at

Master of Law LL.M.s programs are offered by the University of Vienna school of law and at the Vienna University of Economics. Find more information here:

 llm-guide.com

TESTIMONIALS

ALYSSA, 29

creative operations manager

I am currently participating in an online photography course as part of my educational leave (*Bildungskarenz*). Sabbaticals of this kind are a great opportunity to get further education as an adult while still receiving funds to cover your expenses. The amount of education benefits (*Weiterbildungsgeld*) you receive depends on your salary (around 60-80% of your net income). The application process is complicated, so unless you're fluent in German, I'd suggest asking a native speaker for help. To qualify, you must have worked for at least six months and you need a valid residence permit. Verify if your envisaged training fulfills all requirements and that the respective educational institution can confirm this (e.g. the course must be one coherent program – not a combination of several mini-courses – and last between two months and one year, encompassing 20 hours of weekly study time). What's great is that online classes qualify too as long as they include a certain amount of teacher-student interaction. In my case, my employer approached me to discuss the possibility of taking an educational leave, and within just two to three weeks my sabbatical officially started. Still, although being this spontaneous worked for me, I recommend planning ahead of time because it was quite stressful to adapt to the change and to find a course that was accepted by the AMS (see Arbeitsmarktservice, p 152).

KATHI, 37,

self-employed

Many Viennese would love to be self-employed but nevertheless stay in their nine-to-five jobs, letting their dreams fall through. But not me! Thankfully, Vienna provides a lot of support to future entrepreneurs. I relied on a business start-up program (Unternehmensgründungsprogramm) offered by the Public Employment Service Austria (AMS, see p 152) through the company ÖSB Consulting. You can enter this program if you are unemployed and submit an application to the AMS, and once you're in, the program supports you with workshops and monthly coaching appointments, also helping you find mentors and business partners so that you can found a company within six months. Throughout this time, you receive unemployment compensation and can – under certain conditions – take up marginal employment. In my opinion, this program is absolutely unique and valuable, and I would recommend it to all entrepreneurs in the making!

SIMON, 79
advertising and marketing planner

After working as a British-born advertising and marketing planner over many years in Düsseldorf, New York and Frankfurt, I arrived in Vienna in the mid-1990s to continue as a freelancer, working through advertising agencies in Vienna and Prague. At that point, I got the unexpected opportunity to work as a business school lecturer. The Austrian business school landscape was growing fast at this time and with no formal teaching training I was hired sporadically by the Werbeakademie (part of WIFI Wien) and universities to develop and deliver courses on marketing planning (at the diploma, BA and MSc level).

In the last decade, the number of vocational and business school programs has increased enormously. The basic provider is WIFI, the state-supported service and educational arm of the WKO (Austrian chamber of commerce), which has always offered further vocational education in auto mechanics, hairdressing, bookkeeping etc., but has expanded its program to all areas of commerce (such as marketing, PR, cost control, personnel/HR). In fact, many employers say they prefer hiring people from WIFI and universities of applied sciences as they come equipped with real-life work experience and are more disciplined.

A clear trend in recent years has been the expansion of English-language courses on offer. This has the double benefit of equipping Austrian students with good business English and attracting foreign students to broaden the mix.

DIRECTORY

LINKS/CONTACT INFORMATION

SERVICE CENTERS – GENERAL

EXPAT CENTER - VIENNA BUSINESS AGENCY
1., Schmerlingplatz 3
+43 (0)1 400 08 70 91
expatcenter@wirtschaftsagentur.at
info@wirtschaftsagentur.at
English, German and many more

EUROPA BÜRO DER BILDUNGSDIREKTION FÜR WIEN
8., Auerspergerstraße 15/42
+43 (0)1 525 25 -77085
europa@bildung-wien.gv.at

SERVICE CENTERS RELATED TO COMPULSORY SCHOOLING

SCHULINFO WIEN
+43 (0)1 525 25 – 7700
schulinfo@bildung-wien.gv.at

BEGABUNGSFÖRDERUNGSZENTRUM DER BILDUNGSDIREKTION FÜR WIEN
+43 (0)1 525 25 -77887, -77889
begabung@bildung-wien.gv.at

INTEGRATIONSBERATUNGSSTELLE DER BILDUNGSDIREKTION FÜR WIEN
Verena Lieser. +43 (0)1 525 25 -77193,
verena.lieser@bildung-wien.gv.at
Mag.a Judith Stender, +43 (0)1 525 25 -77194,
Judith.stender@bildung-wien.gv.at
Personal appointments upon request

SERVICE CENTERS RELATED TO TERTIARY & ADULT EDUCATION

ADVISORY CENTER FOR MIGRANTS
AST Perspektive – Beratungszentrum für Migranten und Migrantinnen
2., Nordbahnstraße 36/1
+43 (0)585 80 19
ast.wien@migrant.at
perspektive@migrant.at
migrant.at/sprache/english/
English, German

WAFF - CAREERS AND FURTHER EDUCATION ADVISORY CENTER
WAFF - Wiener ArbeitnehmerInnen Förderungsfonds
2., Nordbahnstraße 36/1
+43 (1) 217 480
waff@waff.at, waff.at/en/
English, German and others

TEACHING AFFAIRS AND STUDY SERVICES, UNIVERSITY OF VIENNA
Studienservice und Lehrwesen, Universität Wien]
1., Universitätsring 1
slw.univie.ac.at/en/about-us/admission-office/
Online contact form: slw.univie.ac.at/index. php?id=29578

[BERUFSFÖRDERUNGSINSTITUT, BFI WIEN]
3., Alfred-Dallinger-Platz 1
+43 1 811 78 - 10100
Bfi.wien
information@bfi.wien

[BUNDESINSTITUT FÜR ERWACHSENENBILDUNG, BIFEB]
5360, St. Wolfgang, Bürglstein 1-7
+43 6137 6621-0
office@bifeb.at

WIRTSCHAFTSFÖRDERUNGSINSTITUT, WIFI WIEN
18., Währinger Gürtel 97, +43 1 476 77
wifi.at
Kundenservice@wifiwien.at

DIE WIENER VOLKSHOCHSCHULEN
+43 1 893 00 83
vhs.at
info@vhs.at

PUBLIC EMPLOYMENT SERVICE AUSTRIA
[Arbeitsmarktservice, AMS]
3., Ungargasse 37, +43 1 50 904 940
ams.at

LEGAL AND PSYCHOLOGICAL GUIDANCE & COUNSELLING FOR PARENTS, PUPILS & STUDENTS

PSYCHOLOGICAL COUNSELLING SERVICES FOR STUDENTS IN HIGHER EDUCATION
Psychologische Studierendenberatung Wien
8., Lederergasse 35/4
+43 1 402 30 91
studierendenberatung.at

CONTACT AND HELPDESK OF THE OFFICE FOR FOREIGN STUDENTS
Referat für ausländische Studierende, ÖH
4., Taubstummengasse 7-9
+43 1 310 88 80 65
ar@oeh.ac.at
oeh.ac.at/en/referate/office-forgein-students

FINANCIAL SUPPORT, SCHOLARSHIPS & GRANTS

SCHÜLERBEIHILFE DER BILDUNGSDIREKTION FÜR WIEN]
schulbeihilfen@bildung-wien.gv.at

STUDY GRANT AUTHORITY
Studienbeihilfenbehörde
10., Gudrunstraße 179
+43 1 601 73 0
stipendium.at

SERVICES RELATED TO VOCATIONAL EDUCATION

INFORMATION, ADVICE AND COORDINATION OFFERED BY THE CULTURE AND SPORTS CLUB OF VIENNA'S VOCATIONAL SCHOOLS
Informations-, Beratungs- und Koordinationsstelle des Kultur- und Sportvereins der Wiener Berufsschulen
Mag. Rudol Freyenschlag, Dr. Wolfgang Fronek
+43 1 599 16 95 28 1
Berufsmatura-wien@kusonline.at

SERVICES – GENERAL

EXPAT CENTER - VIENNA BUSINESS AGENCY
7., Mariahilferstraße 20 +43 1 40 00 86 70
info@wirtschaftsagentur.at, viennabusinessagency.at
English, German & 10 other languages

VIENNA BOARD OF EDUCATION
Bildungsdirektion für Wien 1.,
Wipplingerstraße 28
+43 1 52 52 50, office@bildung-wien.gv.at
wien.gv.at/bildung/stadtschulrat/
Mon-Fri 07:30-15:30
German

EUROPEAN OFFICE - VIENNA BOARD OF EDUCATION
Europa Büro der Bildungsdirektion für Wien
8., Auerspergerstraße 15/42
+43 1 52 52 57 70 85, europa@bildung-wien.gv.at
eb.ssr-wien.at
English, German

CHAMBER OF LABOR VIENNA
Arbeiterkammer Wien
4., Prinz Eugen Straße 20-22
+43 1 50 16 50, Online contact form
wien.arbeiterkammer.at
Mon-Fri 08:00-15:45
German

WIENXTRA
7., Museumsplatz 1
+43 1 400 08 44 00, kinderinfowien@wienxtra.at
wienxtra.at
English, German

MUNICIPAL OFFICE FOR INTEGRATION AND DIVERSITY (MA 17)
Magistratsabteilung Integration und Diversität
8., Friedrich-Schmidth-Platz 3
+43 1 400 08 15 10, post@ma17.wien.gv.at
wien.gv.at/kontakte/ma17/
Mon-Fri 07:30-15:30
German

MUNICIPAL OFFICE FOR IMMIGRATION AND CITIZENSHIP (MA 35)
Magistratsabteilung Einwanderung und
Staatsbürgerschaft
20., Dresdner Straße 93 (Block C)
+43 1 40 00 35 35, post@ma35.wien.gv.at
wien.gv.at/kontakt/ma35/
German

SERVICES RELATED TO PRE-SCHOOLS

TAGESELTERNZENTRUM
5., Wehrgasse 26
+43 1 36 8 71 91
beratung@tageselternzentrum.at
tageselternzentrum.at
Mon, Tue, Thu, Fri 09:00-14:00
German

WIENER HILFSWERK
7., Schottenfeldgasse 29
+43 1 512 36 61
info@wiener.hilfswerk.at
hilfswerk.at
German

VOLKSHILFE WIEN
19., Weinberggasse 77
+43 1 36 06 40, sekretariat@volkshilfe-wien.at
volkshife-wien.at
German

VEREIN DER WIENER ELTERNVERWALTETEN KINDERGRUPPEN
6., Hofmühlgasse 2/7
+43 1 585 72 44, office@kindergruppen.at
kindergruppen.at
German

VEREIN WIENER KINDERGRUPPEN
7., Stuckgasse 8/3
+43 681 20 32 92 15, office@wienerkindergruppen.org
wienerkindergruppen.org
German

MUNICIPAL OFFICE FOR YOUTH AND FAMILY (MA 11)
Wiener Kinder- und Jugendhilfe
3., Rüdengasse 11
+43 40 00 80 11, post@ma11.wien.gv.at
wien.gv.at/kontakte/ma11/
German

VIENNA'S MUNICIPAL OFFICE FOR KINDERGARTENS (MA 10)
Magistratsabteilung Wiener Kindergärten
3., Thomas-Klestil-Platz 11
+43 1 400 09 03 09, post@ma10.wien.gv.at
wien.gv.at/kontakte/ma10/

SERVICES RELATED TO COMPULSORY SCHOOLING

SCHULINFO WIEN
1., Wipplingerstraße 28
+43 1 525 25 77 00, chulinfo@bildung-wien.gv.at
Mon, Tue & Thu 08:30-15:00, Fri 08:30-12:00 (personal)
Mon, Tue, Thu & Fri 08:30-15:00 (telephone)
German

BEGABUNGSFÖRDERUNGSZENTRUM DER BILDUNGSDI-REKTION FÜR WIEN
1., Wipplingerstraße 28
+43 1 525 25 77 887, -77 888, -77 889
begabung@bildung-wien.gv.at
bildung-wien.gv.at
German

INTEGRATIONSBERATUNGSSTELLE DER BILDUNGSDIREK-TION FÜR WIEN
Verena Lieser: +43 1 525 25 77 193,
verena.lieser@bildung-wien.gv.at
Mag.a Judith Stender: +43 1 525 25 77194,
Judith.stender@bildung-wien.gv.at
bildung-wien.gv.at
Mon-Fri 08:00-15:00
German

REFERAT FÜR SCHULVERSUCHE UND SCHULENTWICK-LUNG DER BILDUNGSDIREKTION FÜR WIEN
2., Karmelitergasse 9
schulentwicklung.at
German

SERVICES RELATED TO RELIGIOUS SCHOOLS

ISRAELITISCHE KULTUSGEMEINDE WIEN
1., Seitenstettengasse 4
+43 1 53 10 40, office@ikg-wien.at
ikg-wien.at
English, German

ISLAMISCHE GLAUBENSGEMEINSCHAFT IN ÖSTERREICH
7., Bernardgasse 5
+43 1 526 31 22, office@derislam.at
derislam.at
Mon, Wed & Fri 09:00-13:00, Tue & Thu 13:00-16:30
German

SERVICES RELATED TO EXTRA-CURRICULAR ACTIVITIES FOR PUPILS

BILDUNG IM MITTELPUNKT (BIM)
15., Anschützgasse 1
+43 1 52 42 50 90, office@bildung-wien.at
bildung-wien.at
Mon-Thu 08:00-16:00, Fri 08:00-13:30
German

ARBEITSGEMEINSCHAFT FÜR SPORT UND KÖRPERKULTUR (ASKÖ WAT) WIEN
3., Maria Jacobi-Gasse 1, Media Quartier Marx 3.2
+43 1 226 00 17, office@askoewat.wien
askoewat.wien
Mon-Thu 09:00-17:00, Fri 09:00-13:00
German

SPORTUNION WIEN
1., Dominikanerbastei
+43 1 512 74 63, office@sportunion-wien.at
sportunion-wien.at
Mon-Thu 09:00-16:00, Fri 09:00-12:00
German

MUSIC SCHOOLS VIENNA
Musikschule Wien
8., Skodagasse 20
+43 1 400 08 44 10, post-kms@ma13.wien.gv.at
wien.gv.at/kontakte/musikschule/
German

WIENXTRA MEDIENZENTRUM
7., Zieglergasse 49 / II
+43 1 400 08 34 44 , medienzentrum@wienXtra.at
medienzentrum.at
English, German

WIENXTRA SOUNDBASE
8., Friedrich-Schmidth-Platz 5
+ 43 1 400 08 43 85, soundbase@wienxtra.at
soundbase.at
English, German

SUMMER CITY CAMPS
15., Anschützgasse 1
+43 1 524 25 09 46, info@summercitycamp.at
summercitycamp.at
Mon-Thu 09:00-16:00
Fri 09:00-14:00
German

SERVICES RELATED TO TUTORING

DIE WIENER VOLKSHOCHSCHULEN
+43 1 893 00 83, info@vhs.at
vhs.at
German

LERNQUADRAT
6., Mariahilfer Straße 103
+43 1 812 45 45, info@lernquadrat.at
lernquadrat.at
Mon-Sun 00:00-24:00 (hotline)
German

SCHÜLERHILFE
Online contact forms and phone numbers for the individual institutes
schuelerhilfe.at
German

FRIENDS KINDER-, JUGEND- UND FAMILIENZENTRUM
2., Franz-Hochedlinger-Gasse 30-32
+43 1 699 15 05 23 76, info@friends2.at
friends2.at
German

JUHU! JUGENDHILFSWERK DER FAMILIE UMEK – VEREIN ZUR UNTERSTÜTZUNG HILFSBEDÜRFTIGER JUNGER MENSCHEN
12., Fockygasse 33/1a , +43 1 66 07 73 87 66, +43 1 810 41 58
office@vereinjuhu.at
Mon-Wed 10:00-18:30, Thu 10:00-17:30, Fri 10:00-16:30
vereinjuhu.at
German

KONTAKTEPOOL WIEN DER STATION WIEN
5., Einsiedlerplatz 5/7
+43 1 966 80 96, office@stationwien.com
stationwien.org
Mon, Tue & Thu 10:00-16:00, Fri 10:00-15:00
German

CARITAS WIEN
16., Albrechtskreithgasse 19-21
+43 1 87 81 20, office@caritas-wien.at
caritas-wien.at
German

INSTITUTE FOR ECONOMIC DEVELOPMENT VIENNA
Wirtschaftsförderungsinstitut, WIFI Wien
18., Währinger Gürtel 9
+43 1 476 77, Kundenservice@wifiwien.at
wifi.at
German

SERVICES RELATED TO TERTIARY & ADULT EDUCATION

ADVISORY CENTER FOR NON-AUSTRIANS WITH QUALIFICATIONS ACQUIRED ABROAD
AST Wien – Anlaufstelle für Personen mit im Ausland erworbenen Qualifikationen für Wien
2., Nordbahnstraße 36/1
+43 1 585 80 19, ast.wien@migrant.at
migrant.at/sprache/english/
Mon, Tue & Wed 10:00-12:00
Thu 14:00-16:00
English, German

ADVISORY CENTER REGARDING THE RECOGNITION OF QUALIFICATIONS AND FURTHER EDUCATION FOR NON-AUSTRIANS
Perspektive – Anerkennungs- und Weiterbildungsberatungsstelle für NeuzuwanderInnen und Asylberechtigte
2., Nordbahnstraße 36/1
+43 1 585 80 19, perspektive@migrant.at
migrant.at/sprache/english/
Mon, Tue & Wed 10:00-12:00, Thu 14:00-16:00
English, German

ENIC NARIC AUSTRIA - NATIONAL ACADEMIC RECOGNITION CENTER
1., Teinfaltstraße 8
+43 1 531 20 59 20, naric@bmbwf.gv.at
naric.at
English, German

AUSTRIAN EXCHANGE SERVICE
Österreichischer Austauschdienst OeAD
1., Ebendorferstraße 7
+43 1 53 40 84 82, wien@oead.at
oead.at
Mon, Wed & Fri 09:00-12:00, Tue & Thu 10:00-12:00, 14:00-16:00
English, German

WAFF - CAREERS AND FURTHER EDUCATION ADVISORY CENTER
WAFF - Wiener ArbeitnehmerInnen Förderungsfonds
2., Nordbahnstraße 36/1
+43 1 21 74 85 55, +43 1 800 86 86 86 (info hotline)
bbe@waff.at
waff.at/en/
Mon-Thu 09:00-16:00, Fri 09:00-15:00
English, German

TEACHING AFFAIRS AND STUDY SERVICES, UNIVERSITY OF VIENNA

Studienservice und Lehrwesen, Universität Wien
1., Universitätsring 1
Online contact form
slw.univie.ac.at/en/about-us/admission-office/
English, German

VOCATIONAL TRAINING INSTITUT

Berufsförderungsinstitut, BFI Wien
3., Alfred-Dallinger-Platz 1
+43 1 81 17 81 01 00, information@bfi.wien
Bfi.wien
German

FEDERAL INSTITUTE FOR ADULT EDUCATION

Bundesinstitut für Erwachsenenbildung, bifeb
5360, St. Wolfgang, Bürglstein 1-7
+43 6 13 76 62 10, office@bifeb.at
bifeb.at
German

INSTITUTE FOR ECONOMIC DEVELOPMENT VIENNA

Wirtschaftsförderungsinstitut, WIFI Wien
18., Währinger Gürtel 9
+43 1 476 77 55 55, Kundenservice@wifiwien.at
wifi.at
German

DIE WIENER VOLKSHOCHSCHULEN

+43 1 893 00 83, info@vhs.at
vhs.at
German

PUBLIC EMPLOYMENT SERVICE AUSTRIA

Arbeitsmarktservice, AMS
3., Ungargasse 37
+43 1 50 90 49 40 (service line)
Online contact form: ams.at
Mon-Thu 07:30-16:00, Fri 07:30-13:00
German

SERVICES RELATED TO EXTRA-CURRICULAR ACTIVITIES FOR STUDENTS AND ADULTS

UNIVERSITÄTSSPORTINSTITUT WIEN, USI

15., Auf der Schmelz 6a
+43 1 42 77 -17001, -17037, USI@univie.ac.at
usi.at
English, German

AUSTRIAN SPORTS FEDERATION FOR THE DISABLED

Österreichischer Behindertensportverband, ÖBSV
20., Brigittenauer Lände 42
+43 1 332 61 34, office@obsv.at
obs.at
German

VIENNA UNIVERSITY PHILHARMONIC

(Philharmonie Wien)
info@philharmonie.wien
philharmonie.wien
English, German

SERVICES RELATED TO VOCATIONAL EDUCATION

THE CULTURE AND SPORTS CLUB OF VIENNA'S VOCATIONAL SCHOOLS

Kultur- und Sportverein der Wiener
Berufsschulen, KUS
15., Hütteldorfer Straße 7-17
+43 1 52 52 57 73 77, office@kusonline.at
kusonline.at
German

LEGAL AND PSYCHOLOGICAL GUIDANCE AND COUNSELLING

PSYCHOLOGICAL COUNSELLING SERVICES FOR STUDENTS IN HIGHER EDUCATION
Psychologische Studierendenberatung Wien
8., Lederergasse 35/4
+43 1 402 30 91
psychologische.studentenberatung@univie.ac.at
studierendenberatung.at
Mon, Wed & Thu 09:00-12:00, 13:00-15:00
Tue 13:00-15:00, Fri 09:00-12:00
English, German

OFFICE FOR FOREIGN STUDENTS
(Referat für ausländische Studierende, ÖH)
4., Taubstummengasse 7-9
+43 1 310 88 80 65, ar@oeh.ac.at
oeh.ac.at/en/referate/office-forgein-students
English, German

FINANCIAL SUPPORT, SCHOLARSHIPS & GRANTS

EDUCATION ALLOWANCES – VIENNA BOARD OF EDUCATION
Schülerbeihilfe der Bildungsdirektion für Wien
1., Wipplingerstraße 28
+43 1 52 52 50, schulbeihilfen@bildung-wien.gv.at
bildung-wien.gv.at
Mon 13:00-15:00, Tue & Thu 08:30-12:00 (personal)
Tue 07:30-12:00, Thu 12:30-15:30 (telephone)
German

STUDY GRANT AUTHORITY
Studienbeihilfenbehörde
10., Gudrunstraße 179a
+43 1 60 17 30
Online contact form: stipendium.at
Mon, Tue, Wed & Fri 08:00-12:00, 13:00-14:00
German

INFORMATION ON EDUCATIONAL REFORMS

FEDERAL MINISTRY OF EDUCATION, SCIENCE AND RESEARCH
Bildungsministerium für Bildung, Wissenschaft und Forschung
1., Minoritenplatz 5
+43 1 53 12 00, ministerium@bmbwf.gv.at
bmbwf.gv.at
Tue & Thu 09:00-12:00
English, German

GLOSSARY

GERMAN WORD	ENGLISH	SECTION	PAGE
AHS	Allgemein höhere Schule, Academic Secondary School (Gymnasium or Higher General Education School)	Secondary school	125
APS	Allgemeinbildende Pflichtschule, compulsory general schooling (1st to 9th school years)	Primary school	96
Arbeitnehmerfreizügigkeit	Freedom of movement for workers in the European Union	Adult education	231
Arbeitsmarktservice (AMS)	Austrian Public Employment Service; Austria's leading provider of labor-market related services; also offers qualification opportunities and financial assistance	Adult education	252
Aufbaulehrgänge	Advanced training courses which BMS graduates can complete to prepare for taking the Matura	Secondary school	138
Aufenthaltsbewilligung	Residence permit	Adult education	215
Aufnahmebestätigung	Certificate issued by primary school recommending promotion to secondary school (NMS or AHS)	Secondary school	159
Aufnahmeprüfung	Entrance exam. For Academic Secondary School (AHS), usually required when 4th year primary school grades in compulsory courses are lower than "gut" or if a student is matriculating from a non-accredited private/alternative primary school	Secondary school	159
Ausländerbeschäftigungsgesetz (AuslBG)	Law on the Employment of Foreign Nationals	Adult Education	232
Außerordentliche/r Schüler/in	Children who speak very little German allowed to attend primary school and advance to the respective next level, while being granted two years in which they are not graded and can acquire basic German skills	Introduction	19
Außerordentliches Studium	Students who are not admitted to a specific study program but to certain lectures (non-degree program)	Adult education	192
Befriedigend	Satisfactory (as an evaluation mark)	Secondary school	165
Berufsbildende Schule	Vocational school	Secondary school	138
Berufsbildende Höhere Schule (BHS)	Five-year vocational schools which offer higher-level vocational training in areas such as tourism, engineering, business etc. plus a comprehensive general education. The BHS combines job training (also through obligatory internships and training firms) with a higher education entrance examination	Secondary school	140
Berufsbildende Mittlere Schule (BMS)	BMSs are three- or four-year vocational secondary schools which combine basic work-related competences, such as accounting or business studies, with a general education. They do not include a higher education entrance examination.	Secondary school	138
Berufsreifeprüfung (BRP)	BRP ("Berufsmatura") is a required higher-education entrance examination for vocational education pupils and vocational apprentices	Secondary school	152
Beschäftigungsbewilligung	Work permit	Adult Education	232

GERMAN WORD	ENGLISH	SECTION	PAGE
Bildungsdirektion für Wien	Vienna's education board	Introduction	25
Bildungskarenz	Education leave from work	Adult education	246
Bologna Prozess	Bologna Process: a major reform of European higher education in 1999 which introduced ECTS points and the three-partite degree system (bachelor, master, PhD), among other things	Adult education	192
Deutschförderklassen/-kurse	Special German language classes and courses for pupils with little to no prior knowledge of the language, taken together with or parallel to regular school instruction	Bilingual- and English-language schooling	44
Diplomarbeit	Thesis	Secondary school	146
DLP	Dual Language Programme	Bilingual- and English-language schooling	48
Duale Berufsausbildung	The dual vocational education and training program (also called apprenticeship training) combines theoretical training at vocational schools and practical training in a training company	Secondary school	135
ECTS	ECTSs (European Credit Transfer and Accumulation System) are points that are estimated based on the average workload of a university course/lecture. One ECTS point equals about 25 to 30 hours of work.	Adult education	190
Elternabende	Parent-teacher (evening) informational meetings	Primary school	105
Elternbeiträge	Monthly costs for daycare and meals at kindergarten and schools	Pre-school kindergarten	82
Elternverein	Association representing pupils' parents at each school	Secondary school	163
EPS / EMS / EHS	European (Primary, Middle, High) School	Bilingual- and English-language schooling	49
Erhebungsblatt	Application form for enrolling a student in a secondary school (NMS or AHS)	Primary school	117
Erwachsenenbildung	Adult education; in this survival guide, we use this term to refer to all types of personal and career advancement programs available to adults excluding second-chance education	Adult education	245
Erziehungsberech-tigte(n)	Parent(s) or legal guardian(s)	Introduction	11
Essensbeitrag	Monthly costs for meals at kindergarten and school	Pre-school kindergarten	84
Externistenprüfung	Exams held by a commission in a public school evaluating students from alternative education forms (e.g. home schooling, non-accredited schools), for entrance to high schools, as make-up exams in a specific subject, or for the Matura. Also used for AHS students who need a vocational diploma Berufsreifeprüfung	Introduction	22

GERMAN WORD	ENGLISH	SECTION	PAGE
Fachhochschule	Universities of applied sciences; tertiary education institutions which offer degrees that are more hands-on and practically oriented than universities.	Adult education	194
Familiengruppen	Family groups; small groups of up to 22 children of mixed ages (0-6)	Pre-school kindergarten	68
Fenstertag	A day adjacent to an official holiday when some kindergartens and schools are closed (to create a long holiday weekend)	Pre-school kindergarten	25
Ferien	Vacation	Introduction	25
FIP / FIPS	Français intégré à l'école primaire / Français intégré dans les projets au secondaire	Bilingual- and English-language schooling	50
Frühwarnsystem	Early warning system if a pupil is in danger of not passing a grade level. Parents are given opportunities to meet with teachers and for tutoring	Secondary school	166
Ganztagsschulen	All-day schools (combining instruction, study periods and leisure activities until at least 16:00)	Secondary school	132
GEPS	Global Education Primary School	Bilingual- and English-language schooling	48
Grundstufe	Basic level (first two or three years) of primary school	Primary school	98
Gymnasium (G or AkG)	Academic Secondary School (AHS); 5th to 12th school years; academic, university prep, focus on languages (English, Latin +1 living language, usually French)	Secondary school	125
Häuslicher Unterricht	Homeschooling	Secondary school	142
Hort(e)	After-school daycare facility	Secondary school	170
IB	International Baccalaureate (Secondary school diploma offered by some international schools)	Introduction	24
Immatrikulation	Enrollment at a university	Adult education	215
Internat	Boarding school	Secondary school	132
Jahreszeugnis	Final written report pupils receive at the end of the school year (in June/July)	Secondary school	142
JHS	Junior High School	Bilingual- and English-language schooling	49
Klasse	Literally, class. The 1st to 8th Klassen of secondary school are the 5th to 12th school years	Introduction	28
Klausurprüfungen	Proctored (written) exams	Secondary school	147
Kindergruppen	Children's groups self-governed by parents	Pre-school kindergarten	70
Klassenforum	The Klassenforum exists at primary schools/NMS/schools for children with special needs. It is the decision-making and advisory board which includes the main teacher of a class and the pupils' parents	Pre-school kindergarten	23

GERMAN WORD	ENGLISH	SECTION	PAGE
Kleinkindergruppen	Small children's pre-school groups (up to 3 years old)	Pre-school kindergarten	73
Kompensationsprüfungen	Make-up tests	Secondary school	147
KundInnen Nummer	Official registration number from MA 10 needed for enrollment in kindergarten	Pre-school & kindergarten	81
Lehre mit Matura	Apprenticeship-with-Matura model allowing pupils to prepare for and partly take the Matura exams during their apprenticeship training	Secondary school	137
Lehrplan	Curriculum	Introduction	20
MA 10	City of Vienna Municipal Department for Kindergartens	Pre-school kindergarten	81
MA 11	City of Vienna Municipal Department for Youth and Family	Secondary school	172
Magister/ Magistra (Mag./Mag.)	Academic title which used to be awarded to graduates of a 5-year arts degree in Austria and Germany. Most degrees have now switched to the MA system	Adult education	190
Matura	Diploma following successful completion of AHS (Gymnasium) and comprehensive exams (Reifeprüfungen)	Adult education	192
Meisterprüfung	Exam for the master craftsman's diploma	Secondary school	137
Meisterschule	Master Craftsman School, i.e. specialized courses that further deepen the theoretical and practical education of people who have completed an apprenticeship	Secondary school	137
Mehrstufenklassen	Classroom integrating pupils of mixed ages and school years	Primary school	99
Meldebehörde	Registration office	Adult education	215
Mündliche Prüfungen	Oral examinations	Secondary school	147
Muttersprache	Mother tongue / Native language	Bilingual- and English-language schooling	52
Nachhilfe	Tutoring	Secondary school	181
NMS	Neue Mittelschule, New Secondary School	Primary school	116
Nostrifikation	Official recognition of a foreign certificate/degree as equivalent to an Austrian one. May require additional Externistenprüfungen and German Sprachbeherrschungsprüfung	Secondary school	154
Noten	Pupil's evaluation marks, assessed by their teachers Sehr gut (1) = very good Gut (2) = good Befriedigend (3) = satisfactory Genügend (4) = sufficient (passing) Nicht genügend (5) = insufficient (failing)	Primary school	114
Oberstufe	9th to 12th (or 13th) school years (secondary schools)	Secondary school	130
Oberstufen-realgymnasium (ORG)	Realgymnasium offering instruction only from the 9th to 12th school years. Different schools offer different focuses, incl. music, natural sciences, art, informatics, sport	Secondary school	131

GERMAN WORD	ENGLISH	SECTION	PAGE
Ohne Bekenntnis	Without official religious affiliation	Primary school	109
Öffentlichkeitsrecht	Public recognition/accreditation of an educational institution	Secondary school	142
Österreichischer Behindertensportverband (ÖBSV)	Austrian Sports Federation for the Disabled; offers sports courses for people with disabilities	Adult education	235
Österreichische Hochschüler_innenschaft (ÖH)	Austrian National Union of Students federal body of representatives; the official political and legal representative of all students to ministries	Adult education	237
Osterferien	One-and-a-half weeks of school holidays around Easter	Introduction	25
Pädagogik-Paket	The most recent education reform in Austria. The parts of it that have already been ratified include the re-introduction of number grades in primary schools, the achievement-based grouping of students in the NMS, and the addition of a voluntary 10th year of schooling at vocational schools	Introduction	11
Polytechnische Schule	A pre-vocational school at which pupils can complete their final, 9th year of compulsory schooling and become familiar with different vocational opportunities	Secondary school	136
Pfingstferien	Four days of school holidays around Pentecost	Introduction	25
Pflicht(fächer/-gegenstände)	Mandatory courses. Acceptance into AHS requires at least "gut" grades in German, reading, writing and math for the final (4th) year of primary school	Pre-school & kindergarten	159
Pflicht-(schule)	Compulsory schooling in Austria (1st to 9th school years), including primary school and another five years at AHS, NMS or BMS	Primary school	96
Pflichtschulabschluss	Lower secondary school completion certificate	Adult education	247
Private Pflichtschule mit Öffentlich-keitsrecht	Many 'private schools' are actually private schools under public law. They stick to the same curriculum as public schools and their teachers are paid by the city	Introduction	20
Private Pflichtschule ohne Öffentlichkeitsrecht	Private schools which are not officially approbated	Introduction	20
PISA Studie	The PISA (Programme for International Student Assessment) study, an international OECD study that compares educational systems every three years	Introduction	15
Realgymnasium (Rg)	Academic Secondary School (5th to 12th school years) with focus on math, science, linear drawing, technical/textile handwork, or on creative arts	Secondary school	126
Reifeprüfung	Comprehensive exams (oral and written) required for Matura diploma	Secondary school	130
Rot-Weiß-Rot Karte	Red-White-Red Card; once you have graduated from a master's degree or the second stage of a diploma degree at an Austrian tertiary education institution, you can apply for another type of residence title, the Red-White-Red-Card. For this you need to fulfil certain requirements: e.g. your job must correspond to your level of education and you must earn a monthly gross salary of € 2,241	Adult education	221
Schnupper-(kurs/stunde)	Free or reduced rate trial session for tutoring or extracurricular activities	Introduction	12

GERMAN WORD	ENGLISH	SECTION	PAGE
Schulautonomie	Leeway given to public schools for diverse lesson plans and periods of instruction	Primary school	99
Schulforum	The Schulforum exists at primary schools/NMS schools/schools for children with special needs. It includes the headteacher, all other teachers and parents functioning as spokespeople for each class. It is the advisory and decision board for the school	Introduction	23
Schüler/-in	Pupil in the 1st to 12th school years (see Student: university level students are called "Student" or "Studierende"	Introduction	19
Schule für Gesundheits- und Krankenpflege	Schools for healthcare and nursing. Until 2023, they will offer a three-year training program in qualified nursing care. After 2023, they will offer training in assistant nursing only	Secondary school	139
Schulführer	A guide and listing of schools (in print and online)	Primary school	104
Schulpflicht	Compulsory education. In Austria, 9 years of compulsory schooling are mandatory	Introduction	14
Schulreif	Readiness of a pupil to attend a primary or advanced school	Pre-school & kindergarten	88
Schulstufe	School year: 1st to 4th = primary school ("Volksschule"); 5th to 12th/13th = secondary school (Mittelschule & höhere Schule)	Secondary school	126
Schultüte	A ceremonial cone filled with goodies traditionally given to pupils on their first day of primary school	Primary school	106
Schulversuche	Experimental pedagogic or organizational school initiatives (see Schulautonomie)	Primary school	99
Schwerpunkt-schule	A secondary school with a special subject emphasis	Secondary school	134
Semesterferien	One week of school holidays at the end of the winter term (in February)	Introduction	25
Semesterzeugnis	Written report pupils receive at the end of the winter term (in February)	Secondary school	164
Seminar	Courses at university with mandatory attendance; concludes with a written paper	Adult education	194
SIB	Scuola Elementare Italiana Bilingue	Bilingual- and English-language schooling	50
SIM	Spanisch in der Mittelschule	Bilingual- and English-language schooling	50
Sommerferien	Nine weeks of school holidays in summer	Introduction	25
Sommersemester	Summer term (usually at university)	Adult education	228
Sonderschule/- kindergarten	Kindergarten or school for children with special needs	Secondary school	134
Sportverein	Sports club	Adult education	225
Spracbeherrschungs- prüfung	An exam to determine if a foreign diploma holder's German is good enough to be granted an equivalent Austrian diploma status (see Nostrifikation)	Secondary school	155

GERMAN WORD	ENGLISH	SECTION	PAGE
Sprechstunde	Extracurricular times when a teacher is available for one-on-one discussions with pupils or parents	Primary school	116
Stadtschulrat	City Board of Education (now renamed Bildungsdirektion für Wien)	Secondary school	142
Student/-in	Tertiary level student (university, college, post-graduate)	Introduction	28
Studienberechtigungs-prüfung (SBP)	Limited higher education entrance examination; you do the SBP with the aim of applying for one specific course of study	Adult education	250
Studieneingangs- und Orientierungsphase (STEOP)	Introductory and Orientation Period; in this first semester of many university degrees, students need to pass a number of exams (they comprise 8-20 ETCS) to be able to continue with their studies	Adult education	222
Tagesbetreuung	"Hort"; Public or private extra-curricular day care	Secondary school	172
Tagesmutter / Tagesvater	Registered childminder caring for up to five toddlers in his or her own home (private form of pre-school childcare)	Pre-school & kindergarten	72
Tag der offenen Tür	Yearly open house days held by schools on which parents and children can visit and get to know the schools	Introduction	29
Tag der Wiener Schulen	The Day of Viennese Schools is a day in early or mid-October on which parents and children can visit Vienna's 670 schools	Introduction	29
Titelwahn	The Austrian obsession with academic and professional titles	Introduction	12
Universitätslehrgang	(Postgraduate) continuing education courses offered by universities	Adult education	253
Universitätssportinstitut (USI)	University sports institute; part of the University of Vienna; offers around 120 different types of sports courses for very affordable prices to students and former students	Adult education	235
Unterstufe	5th to 8th school years at Academic Secondary School or New Secondary School (AHS or NMS). Generally the same system for the 5th and 6th school years	Secondary school	126
Unverbindliche Übungen	Elective extracurricular courses		52
(VBS)	Vienna Bilingual Schools	Bilingual- and English-language schooling	46
Volkshochschule (VHS)	Adult education learning centers	Secondary school	185
Volksschule	Primary/elementary school (1st to 4th school years)	Primary school	95
Vorschule	Pre-school instruction at a primary school. In Austria, an alternative if a pupil is not Schulreif (does not meet qualifications for admission to primary school)	Primary school	98
Vorlesung	University lectures without mandatory attendance	Adult education	197
Vorwissen-schaftliche Arbeit (VWA)	One of three pillars of the Matura exam, VWA consists of a thesis, its presentation and defence	Adult education	197
Vorzeitige Aufnahme	Early admission (to primary school before it is compulsory)	Pre-school & kindergarten	88
Übung	Courses at university with mandatory attendance; include regular assignments and exercises	Adult education 1	197

GERMAN WORD	ENGLISH	SECTION	PAGE
Wahlpflicht-(fächer/-ge-genstände)	Elective courses during the 11th and 12th school years at Academic Secondary Schools (AHS Oberstufe) allowing students to select individualized instruction	Secondary school	130
Wanderarbeiter	Workers who migrate to pursue work, usually without seeking permanent residence	Adult education	226
Wiener Bildungspass	Vienna education booklet; a record of all the language courses, information modules, counseling services and education and further training programs that you attend	Adult education	230
Wiener Sprachgutschein	Vienna language voucher; if you meet specific requirements, the City of Vienna will subsidize your German language courses with up to €300	Adult education	230
Wintersemester	Winter term (usually at university)	Adult education	228
Wirtschaftskundliches Realgym-nasium	Academic Secondary School (5th to 12th school years) with focus on business and economics	Secondary school	126
WMS	Wiener Mittelschule (alternate form of NMS)	Secondary school	133
Zentralmatura	Standardized comprehensive secondary school leaving examination	Secondary school	146
(Jahres-)- Zeugnis	(Annual) report card, certificate of completion	Secondary school	164
Ziffernnote	Number grades (usually between 1 highest grade and 5 lowest grade)	Introduction	14
Zulassungsbescheid	Notification of approval for admission at a university	Adult education	215
Zulassungsdekret	Decree permitting a pupil to undergo an external higher-education entrance examination (Externistenprüfung)	Secondary school	151
Zulassungsprüfungen	Examinations in specific subjects to determine eligibility to take the Reifeprüfungen or Diplomprüfungen	Secondary school	151
Zusatzprüfung	Make-up exam for students receiving satisfactory marks in compulsory subjects. Required for advancement to further education levels	Secondary school	151
Zweiter Bildungsweg	Second-chance education; in this guide, we use this term to refer to catching up on educational qualifications	Adult education	245
Zwickeltage	Also called Fenstertage; extra days scheduled to be bridging days between two holidays	Introduction	29

SOURCES

GETTING STARTED

AUSTRIAN FEDERAL MINISTRY OF EDUCATION, SCIENCE AND RESEARCH, P 14, 18, 43

bildung.bmbwf.gv.at/schulen/bw/ueberblick/sw_oest.html

bildung.bmbwf.gv.at/schulen/service/pb.html

Federal Ministry of Education, Science and Research Statistical Guide 2017

KARRIERE.SN.AT, P 16

karriere.sn.at/karriere-ratgeber/fort-weiterbildung/wo-der-titel-regiert-28942096

kurier.at/leben/titelunwesen-bis-beamtentum-was-von-der-monarchie-blieb/172.522.259

WIENERZEITUNG, P 16

wienerzeitung.at/nachrichten/kultur/mehr-kultur/1000862-Dero-Hochwohlloeblichkeit.html

BIFIE, P 18, 21, 24

bifie.at/wp-content/uploads/2019/04/NBB_2018_Band1_v4_final.pdf (page 32, 37, 79, 142, 144)

OECD, P 19, 20, 25

oecd-ilibrary.org/docserver/9789264266490-en.pdf?expires=1567858619&id=id&accname=guest&checksum=749AA82292F1C462707D25B7A3F8C4AB

oecd.org/pisa/pisa-2015-results-in-focus.pdf (page 5)

oecd-ilibrary.org/docserver/9789264267510-en.pdf?expires=1567860699&id=id&accname=guest&checksum=BD12DC52233B17687C35E15148CC82E2

DIE PRESSE, P 19, 24

diepresse.com/home/bildung/schule/5129816/PISAErgebnis-inakzeptabel_Jeder-Dritte-ist-Risikoschueler

diepresse.com/home/bildung/schule/5181466/Acht-Mythen-zur-Privatschule

SCHULPSYCHOLOGIE.AT, P 22, 23

http://www.schulpsychologie.at/fileadmin/upload/bildungsinformation/bwwillkomm_engl.pdf

CHAMBER OF LABOR UPPER AUSTRIA, P 23

ooe.arbeiterkammer.at/beratung/bildung/schule/vorundvolksschule/Ausserordentliche_Schueler_-innen.html

LEGAL INFORMATION SYSTEM OF THE FEDERAL GOVERNMENT, P 24

ris.bka.gv.at/GeltendeFassung.wxe?Abfrage=Bundesnormen&Gesetzesnummer=10009266

VIENNA INTERNATIONAL SCHOOL, P 25

vis.ac.at/fileadmin/user_upload/VIS/Admissions/VIS_Terms_and_Conditions_19-20.pdf

WIEN.GV, P 12, 26, 29, 46, 52, 53

wien.gv.at/bildung/stadtschulrat/beratung/externisten/haeuslicher-unterricht.html

wien.gv.at/bildung/stadtschulrat/beratung/schulferien.html

wien.gv.at/bildung/stadtschulrat/tag-der-wiener-schulen.html

wien.gv.at/bildung/stadtschulrat/offene-tuer/

wien.gv.at/bildung/stadtschulrat/schulsystem/vbs.html

wien.gv.at/bildung/stadtschulrat/schulsystem/vbs-mittelschule.html

schulentwicklung.at/joomla/images/stories/Sprachinitiativen/Fremdsprachenmodell_SJ_16_17.pdf p. 1-3

wien.gv.at/bildung/stadtschulrat/schulsystem/ahs/muttersprachlicher-unterricht.html

wien.gv.at/english/education/internatschool.htm

DER STANDARD, P 26

derstandard.at/story/2000086283692/immer-mehr-eltern-schicken-ihre-kinder-nicht-in-die-schule

JUSLINE, P 27

jusline.at/gesetz/lbv/paragraf/14

PRINCETON UNIVERSITY OF GERMAN, P 28

german.princeton.edu/wp-content/uploads/2014/11/GPA-Conversion-Chart.pdf

WIKIPEDIA-GRADING SYSTEM FRANCE, P 28

en.wikipedia.org/wiki/Grading_systems_by_country#France

SCHULFERIEN.ORG, P 29

schulferien.org/oesterreich/ferien/2020/

BILDUNGSSYSTEM.AT, P 35

bildungssystem.at/en/

OESTERREICH.GV, P 44

oesterreich.gv.at/themen/bildung_und_neue_medien/schule/Seite.110005.html

SCHULENTWICKLUNG, P 48, 50

schulentwicklung.at/joomla/content/category/17/55/110/

schulentwicklung.at/joomla/content/category/17/67/110/

schulentwicklung.at/joomla/images/stories/Sprachinitiativen/Fremdsprachenmodell_SJ_16_17.pdf p. 14-17

GLOBAL EDUCATION PRIMARY SCHOOL WALTERGASSE, P 48

geps20.schule.wien.at/unsere-schule/geps/vs-huetteldorf.at/?page_id=127

STADTSCHULRAT, P 50

stadtschulrat.at/fileadmin/user_upload/Schwerpunkte/Bilingualit%C3%A4t/andere_Sprachen/SIM.pdf

CHILDREN'S EDUCATION

VIENNA INTERNATIONAL SCHOOL, P 54, 111

vis.ac.at/about-us/vis-story

vis.ac.at/fileadmin/user_upload/VIS/Admissions/VIS_Terms_and_Conditions_19-20.pdf

WIEN.GV, P 67, 68, 75-84, 86, 88, 98, 101, 105, 111-115

wien.gv.at/bildung/kindergarten/staedtisches-angebot/fakten.html

wien.gv.at/recht/landesrecht-wien/rechtsvorschriften/html/s2600100.htm § 3. (1)

wien.gv.at/amtshelfer/gesellschaft-soziales/magelf/bewilligungsverfahren/kindergartenjahr.html

wien.gv.at/menschen/kind-familie/servicestellen/integration.html

wien.gv.at/bildung/kindergarten/platzsuche/kundennummer-anmeldung/index.html

wien.gv.at/bildung/kindergarten/platzsuche/kundennummer-anmeldung/kriterien.html

wien.gv.at/amtshelfer/kultur/bildung/bildungseinrichtungen/foerderung/ausserhalb-wiens.html

wien.gv.at/amtshelfer/gesellschaft-soziales/magelf/finanzielles/essensbeitrag.html

wien.gv.at/bildung/stadtschulrat/schulsystem/pflichtschulen/anmeldung.html

wien.gv.at/statistik/bildung/kinderbetreuung/index.html#daten

wien.gv.at/bildung/stadtschulrat/schulsystem/pflichtschulen/volksschule.html wien.gv.at/bildung/stadtschulrat/

wien.gv.at/bildung/stadtschulrat/beratung/externisten/haeuslicher-unterricht.html

wien.gv.at/bildung/kindergarten/pdf/elternbeitrag-staedtischer-hort.pdf

wien.gv.at/bildung/schulen/schulsachenkauf.html

wien.gv.at/bildung/stadtschulrat/schulsystem/pflichtschulen/schuelerunterstuetzungen.html

wien.gv.at/bildung/stadtschulrat/schulsystem/pflichtschulen/alternative-lernformen.html

wien.gv.at/bildung/stadtschulrat/schulsystem/pflichtschulen/uebertritt.html

FALTER, P 70

falter.at/the-vienna-review/2011/keys-to-the-city-nov-2011

VINDOBINI, P 71

vindobini.at/de/intern:27/historisches

DAY PARENT CENTER, P 72

tageselternzentrum.at/beruf-tageseltern/

tageselternzentrum.at/kosten-und-unterstuetzung/

WIENER.KINDERGRUPPEN, P 73

wiener.kindergruppen.at/?page_id=9

KINDERGARTEN.AT, P 85

kindergarten.at/de/boxarticleshow2-steuerliche-absetzbarkeit-von-kinderbetreuung

SCHULE.AT, P 89

schule.at/portale/volksschule/wochenthemen/detail/schulreife.html

BILDUNGSSYSTEM.AT, P 89

bildungssystem.at/volksschule/vorschule/

OESTERREICH.GV, P 89, 105

oesterreich.gv.at/themen/bildung_und_neue_medien/schule/4/Seite.110033.html

oesterreich.gv.at/themen/bildung_und_neue_medien/schule/4/Seite.110031.html

elternbrief.at/upload/622_Broschuere%20Schulleitung%20bmbf.pdf

STATISTIK AUSTRIA, P 98, 102

statistik-austria.at/wcm/idc/idcplg?IdcService=GET_PDF_FILE&RevisionSelectionMethod=LatestReleased&d DocName=020961

statistik-austria.at/web_de/statistiken/menschen_und_gesellschaft/bildung/schulen/schulbesuch/020953.html

Statistik Austria „Klassenschülerzahlen im Schuljahr 2017/18 nach detaillierten Ausbildungsarten"

statistik-austria.at/wcm/idc/idcplg?IdcService=GET_PDF_FILE&RevisionSelectionMethod= LatestReleased&d DocName=020959

GESCHICHTEWIKI.WIEN.GV, P 99

geschichtewiki.wien.gv.at/Schulversuche

STADT WIEN, P 100

stadt-wien.at/bildung/schule/privatschulen-wien.html

INSTITUTE NEULANDSCHULEN, P 110

nls.at/fileadmin/grinzing/vs/Grafiken/Schulgeld_18.pdf

THERESIANUM, P 110

theresianum.ac.at/data/files/VIT/Downloads/vit_ausbildungsvertrag_19.20.pdf §III(1)

ASTRID LINDGREN ZENTRUM, P 110

astrid-lindgren-zentrum.at/schule/#schule_kosten

SCHULPSYCHOLOGIE.AT, P 114

schulpsychologie.at/fileadmin/upload/bildungsinformation/bwwillkomm_engl.pdf §2

STADTSCHULRAT, P 117

evw.schule.wien.at/fileadmin/s/evw/system/user_upload/ER302_100094_177_2017_Erhebungsblaetter_Leerformul.pdf

TEENAGER EDUCATION

DER STANDARD, P 118

derstandard.at/story/2000089915701/bildung-wird-laut-oecd-in-oesterreich-weiter-ueberdurchschnittlich-vererbt

WIEN.GV, P 126, 130-134, 142, 150, 151, 154, 159, 160, 166-169, 172-174, 177

wien.gv.at/bildung/stadtschulrat/schulsystem/ahs/schultypen.html

bildungssystem.at/schule-oberstufe/allgemein-bildende-hoehere-schule-oberstufe/

wien.gv.at/bildung/stadtschulrat/schulsystem/ahs/schultypen.html

wien.gv.at/bildung/stadtschulrat/schulsystem/pflichtschulen/ganztagsbetreuung.html

wien.gv.at/bildung/stadtschulrat/schulsystem/pflichtschulen/neue-mittelschule.html

wien.gv.at/bildung/stadtschulrat/schulsystem/pflichtschulen/sonder-integration.html

wien.gv.at/bildung/stadtschulrat/beratung/externisten/haeuslicher-unterricht.html

wien.gv.at/bildung/stadtschulrat/beratung/externisten/index.html

wien.gv.at/bildung/stadtschulrat/beratung/externisten/einzelner-unterrichtsgegenstand.html

wien.gv.at/bildung/stadtschulrat/beratung/externisten/externistenreifepruefung.html

wien.gv.at/bildung/stadtschulrat/beratung/externisten/nostrifikationen.html

wien.gv.at/bildung/stadtschulrat/schulsystem/ahs/aufnahme-unterstufe.html

wien.gv.at/bildung/stadtschulrat/schulsystem/ahs/aufnahme-oberstufe.html

wien.gv.at/bildung/stadtschulrat/schulsystem/pflichtschulen/schuelerunterstuetzungen.html

wien.gv.at/bildung/stadtschulrat/schulsystem/pflichtschulen/neue-mittelschule.html

wien.gv.at/bildung/stadtschulrat/schulsystem/ahs/fruehwarnsystem.html

wien.gv.at/amtshelfer/kultur/bildung/bildungseinrichtungen/kinder/hort.html

wien.gv.at/bildung/kindergarten/pdf/elternbeitrag-staedtischer-hort.pdf

wien.gv.at/amtshelfer/gesellschaft-soziales/magelf/finanzielles/essensbeitrag.html

wien.gv.at/menschen/kind-familie/ahs-info/pdf/info-essen-englisch.pdf

wien.gv.at/amtshelfer/kultur/musikschule/anmeldung/ausbildung.html

wien.gv.at/bildung/schulen/musikschule/unterrichtsfaecher/index.html

wien.gv.at/bildung/schulen/musikschule/unterrichtsgebuehren/index.html

BILDUNGSSYSTEM.AT, P 126, 136, 138-140, 152, 153

bildungssystem.at/schule-unterstufe/allgemein-bildende-hoehere-schule-unterstufe/

bildungssystem.at/en/school-upper-secondary/pre-vocational-school/

bildungssystem.at/en/school-upper-secondary/part-time-vocational-school-and-apprenticeship/

bildungssystem.at/en/school-upper-secondary/school-for-intermediate-vocational-education/

bildungssystem.at/en/school-upper-secondary/school-for-intermediate-vocational-education/

bildungssystem.at/en/health-professions/school-of-nursing/

bildungssystem.at/en/school-upper-secondary/college-for-higher-vocational-education/

bildungssystem.at/en/higher-education-entrance-examination/

BEWEGUNGSERZIEHUNG.AT, P 134

bewegungserziehung.at/service/schwerpunktschulen/schwerpunktschulen-details/

IBW AUSTRIA - RESEARCH & DEVELOPMENT IN VET, P 134, 136, 138, 140

ibw.at/en/vocational-education-in-austria/

OESTERREICH.GV, P 136, 138, 140, 146, 147, 152, 153

oesterreich.gv.at/themen/bildung_und_neue_medien/schule/2/Seite.1760130.html

oesterreich.gv.at/themen/bildung_und_neue_medien/schule/2/Seite.1760130.html

oesterreich.gv.at/themen/bildung_und_neue_medien/schule/2/Seite.1760130.html

oesterreich.gv.at/themen/bildung_und_neue_medien/schule/2/Seite.1760140.html

oesterreich.gv.at/themen/bildung_und_neue_medien/schule/2/Seite.1760150.html

oesterreich.gv.at/themen/bildung_und_neue_medien/schule/2/1.html

oesterreich.gv.at/themen/bildung_und_neue_medien/schule/2/1/Seite.110037.html#Vorwissenschaftliche%20Arbeit

oesterreich.gv.at/themen/bildung_und_neue_medien/schule/2/1/Seite.110038.html#Diplomarbeit

oesterreich.gv.at/themen/bildung_und_neue_medien/schule/2/1/Seite.110037.html#Klausurpr%C3%BCfung

oesterreich.gv.at/themen/bildung_und_neue_medien/schule/2/1/Seite.110038.html#M%C3%BCndlich

oesterreich.gv.at/themen/bildung_und_neue_medien/lehre/Seite.333905.html#AllgemeineInformationen

oesterreich.gv.at/themen/bildung_und_neue_medien/lehre/Seite.333905.html#Voraussetzungen

oesterreich.gv.at/themen/bildung_und_neue_medien/lehre/Seite.333905.html#Verfahrensablauf

AUSBILDUNGSKOMPASS.AT. P 137

ausbildungskompass.at/en/

AUSTRIAN ECONOMIC CHAMBER, P 137

wko.at/service/bildung-lehre/lehre-matura.html

wko.at/service/bildung-lehre/LehreundMatura_Bundeslaender.html

BERUFSBILDENDESCHULEN.AT, P 138, 141

abc.berufsbildendeschulen.at/allgemeine-informationen/pflichtpraktikum/

abc.berufsbildendeschulen.at/kollegs-und-kollegs-fuer-berufstaetige/

WIENXTRA, P 156, 177, 178, 184

wienxtra.at/jugendinfo/infos-von-a-z/schulbesuch-im-ausland/

wienxtra.at/

wienxtra.at/medienzentrum/jugendliche/ueber-uns/

wienxtra.at/soundbase/

wienxtra.at/jugendinfo/infos-von-a-z/lern-und-nachhilfe/#c31834

SCHULE-GESCUHT.AT, P 159, 160

schule-gesucht.at/de/tipps-uebersicht/entscheidung/

schule-gesucht.at/de/tipps-uebersicht/daten-fakten/ Statistisches Jahrbuch der Stadt Wien 2018

schule-gesucht.at/de/tipps-uebersicht/entscheidung/

AUSTRIAN LAW, P 159

Schulorganisationsgesetz § 40(1)

BEWEGUNGSERZIEHUNG.AT, P 166

bewegungserziehung.at/sportwochen/rechtlicher-rahmen/verpflichtung-zu-sportwochen/

BILDUNG-WIEN.AT, P 171, 176

bildung-wien.at/home/ueber-uns/geschichte

bildung-wien.at/

KINDERGARTEN.AT, P 175

kindergarten.at/de/boxarticleshow2-steuerliche-absetzbarkeit-von-kinderbetreuung (LStR 2002, Lohnsteuerrichtlinien 2002 §12.7.6)

KINDERFREUNDE WIEN, P 177, 180

wien.kinderfreunde.at/Bundeslaender/Wien

wien.kinderfreunde.at/Bundeslaender/Wien/Unser-Angebot/Ferien/Sommer/Sommerakademien-2019-komm-sei-dabei

wien.kinderfreunde.at/Bundeslaender/Wien/Unser-Angebot/Ferien/Anmeldung

KINDERUNI, P 180

kinderuni.at

KINDERUNIKUNST, P 180

kinderunikunst.at/de

SUMMER CITY CAMP, P 182

summercitycamp.at/infos/

VOLKSHOCHSCHULE, P 182, 187

vhs.at/files/downloads/NUwclBrf36zurYyOm6DG9MBG9XOm4bb89VG5zfgR.pdf

vhs.at/de/kurse

vhs.at/de/e/gratis-lernhilfe

LERNTIPP.AT, P 183

lerntipp.at/eltern/Nachhilfe-Checklisten.shtml

Average price for Vienna also listed on betreut.at as €15,18

NACHHILFEN24.AT, P 186

nachhilfen24.at/de/pages/conditions

UNIJOBS., P 186

unijobs.at/stellenanbieter#preisliste

ADULT EDUCATION

WIEN.GV, P 188, 200, 231

wien.gv.at/english/social/integration/arriving/start-wien-migrants/language-vouchers.html

wien.gv.at/statistik/pdf/wieninzahlen-2018.pdf

wien.gv.at/english/social/integration/arriving/start-wien-migrants/language-vouchers.html

OESTERREICH.GV, P 192, 193, 211, 216, 219, 223, 224, 226, 229, 232, 246

oesterreich.gv.at/themen/bildung_und_neue_medien/universitaet/Seite.160125.html

oesterreich.gv.at/themen/bildung_und_neue_medien/universitaet/1/2/1/Seite.160363.html

oesterreich.gv.at/themen/bildung_und_neue_medien/universitaet/1/2/1/Seite.160361.html

oesterreich.gv.at/themen/bildung_und_neue_medien/fachhochschulen/Seite.810400.html

oesterreich.gv.at/themen/bildung_und_neue_medien/fachhochschulen/Seite.810200.html

oesterreich.gv.at/themen/bildung_und_neue_medien/universitaet/1/2/Seite.160209.html

oesterreich.gv.at/themen/bildung_und_neue_medien/universitaet/1/2/Seite.160210.html

oesterreich.gv.at/themen/bildung_und_neue_medien/universitaet/1/2/Seite.160208.html oesterreich.gv.at/themen/bildung_und_neue_medien/universitaet/5/Seite.160105.html

oesterreich.gv.at/themen/bildung_und_neue_medien/universitaet/1/2/1/Seite.160367.html

oesterreich.gv.at/themen/bildung_und_neue_medien/universitaet/1/2/1/Seite.160364.html

oesterreich.gv.at/themen/bildung_und_neue_medien/universitaet/1/2/1/Seite.160366.html

oesterreich.gv.at/themen/bildung_und_neue_medien/universitaet/1/2/Seite.160211.html

oesterreich.gv.at/themen/bildung_und_neue_medien/universitaet/1/1/Seite.160224.html

oesterreich.gv.at/themen/arbeit_und_pension/bildungskarenz_und_bildungsteilzeit.html

TIMESHIGHEREDUCATION.COM, P 198

timeshighereducation.com/world-university-rankings/2019/world-ranking#!/page/0/length/25/locations/AT/sort_by/rank/sort_order/asc/cols/stats

FINANCIAL TIMES, P 198

Financial Times ‚European Business School Ranking‘

OEAD, P 198, 218, 219, 228, 232, 233

oead.at/en/news/article/2019/02/qs-subject-ranking-six-austrian-universities-among-the-top-50/

oead.at/en/to-austria/university-preparation-programmes/

oead.at/fileadmin/Dokumente/oead.at/KIM/Nach_Oesterreich/Einreise_und_Aufenthalt/Informationsbroschueren/Englisch/Leitfaden_fuer_internationale_Studierende_en.pdf

oead.at/en/outgoing/#

oead.at/de/ins-ausland/hochschulen/vorbereitung-fuer-studierende/

oead.at/en/to-austria/entry-and-residence/visa-c-or-visa-d/#working

oead.at/en/to-austria/entry-and-residence/residence-permit-student-no-mobility-programme/#working

TOPUNIVERSITIES.COM, P 199

topuniversities.com/university-rankings/university-subject-rankings/2019/performing-arts

STUDY IN AUSTRIA, P 202

studyinaustria.at/de/studium/hochschulen/universitaeten/tu-wien-vienna-university-of-technology/

DIE PRESSE, P 205

diepresse.com/home/bildung/universitaet/5168075/Schauspiel-am-selektivsten

DER STANDARD, P 205

derstandard.at/story/2000065242114/wie-ist-es-kunst-zu-studieren

derstandard.at/story/1350258624059/mehr-bewerber-denn-je-an-akademie-der-bildenden-kuenste

AK BILD, P 205

akbild.ac.at/portal_en/studies/studieninfos_en/language-competency/german-language-courses

BILDUNGSSYSTEM.AT, P 211, 214, 233, 218, 244, 245, 247, 250, 253

bildungssystem.at/en/tertiary-education/university-of-applied-sciences/

bildungssystem.at/en/tertiary-education/university-colleges-of-teacher-education/

bildungssystem.at/en/footer-boxen/guidance-in-austria/guidance-institutions-and-counselors/

bildungssystem.at/en/tertiary-education/university-of-applied-sciences/

bildungssystem.at/en/adult-education/

bildungssystem.at/en/second-chance-education/

bildungssystem.at/en/limited-higher-education-entrance-examination/

bildungssystem.at/en/teriary-education/continuing-education-courses-at-universities-universities-of-applied-sciences-and-university-colleges-of-teacher-education/

bildungssystem.at/en/short-cycle-tertiary-education/school-for-people-in-employment/

bildungssystem.at/en/short-cycle-tertiary-education/post_secondary-vct-course/

STUDIEREN.AT, P 212, 218

studieren.at/fachhochschule/#abschl%C3%BCsse

studieren.at/zulassung/aufnahmeverfahren/#fh

NOE.gv, P 213

noe.gv.at/noe/Wissenschaft-Forschung/Universitaeten_Fachhochschulen.html

AUSTRIAN FEDERAL MINISTRY OF EDUCATION, SCIENCE AND RESEARCH, P 225, 250

bmbwf.gv.at/studium/academic-mobility/enic-naric-austria/

bildung.bmbwf.gv.at/schulen/bw/zb/berufsreifepruefung.html

RECOGNITION INFORMATION APPLICATION SYSTEM, P 225

aais.at/Home/AssessmentOfProfession

FACHHOCHSCHULEN.AC, P 226

fachhochschulen.ac.at/de/fh_studium/2008/studiengebuehren

GRANTS.AT, P 227

grants.at/en/

STIPENDIUM.AT, P 227

stipendium.at/fileadmin/download/PDF/english_information/Studienfoerderung_Englisch_November_2018.pdf

CEEPUS.INFO, P 228

ceepus.info/#nbb

SOCIAL SECURITY, P 229

sozialversicherung.at/expert/enb.cgi?SHOWMODE=1&WIZARD=S-STUDENTEN&TRAEGER=EN&BEREICH=SV&LAYOUT=STYL
EGUIDE&LANG=EN&LAYOUT=HELP

VIENNA REGIONAL HEALTH INSURANCE FUND, P 229

wgkk.at/cdscontent/?contentid=10007796028

WIENXTRA, P 230

wienxtra.at/jugendinfo/infos-von-a-z/info-tag/deutsch-fuer-internationale-schueler-innen-und-
studierendegerman-for-international-students/

STUDENT COUNSELING, P 233, 239

studierendenberatung.at/en/coming-to-a-new-country/

UNIVERSITY SPORTS INSTITUTE VIENNA, P 236, 246

usi.at/en/waff – Vienna Employment Promotion Fund, p

VIENNA EMPLOYMENT PROMOTION FUND, P 246

waff.at/foerderungen/bildungskonto/

CHAMBER OF LABOR VIENNA, P 246, 247

wien.arbeiterkammer.at/service/broschueren/Bildung/Bildungsgutschein_2019.pdf

arbeiterkammer.at/beratung/bildung/zweiterbildungsweg/Pflichtschulabschluss_nachholen.html

ADULT EDUCATION, P 250

erwachsenenbildung.at/bildungsinfo/zweiter_bildungsweg/studienberechtigungspruefung.php

ECONOMIC DEVELOPMENT INSTITUTE OF THE VIENNA ECONOMIC CHAMBER, P 251

wifi.at/start

PUBLIC EMPLOYMENT SERVICE AUSTRIA, P 251, 252

ams.at/organisation/public-employment-service-austria

ams.at/organisation/public-employment-service-austria/about-ams

PROFESSIONAL DEVELOPMENT INSTITUTE, P 251

bfi.wien/

ADULT EDUCATION CENTERS, P 251, 252

vhs.at/de

vhs.at/de/kurse

FEDERAL INSTITUTE FOR ADULT EDUCATION, P 251

bifeb.at/

EUROPEAN COMMISSION, P 251

ec.europa.eu/programs/erasmus-plus/opportunities/individuals/staff-training/adult-education_en

POSTGRADUATECENTER, P 253, 254

postgraduatecenter.at/

postgraduatecenter.at/en/programs/law/european-and-international-business-law/llm-program-english/

EXECUTIVEACADEMY, P 253

executiveacademy.at/de/program/universitaetslehrgaenge/

UNIVERSITIES IN AND AROUND VIENNA, P 194, 197, 201-210, 212, 213, 215, 217, 226, 237, 252

VMI - VIENNA MUSIC INSTITUTE
vmi.at/index_en.html

University of Vienna, Studies Service Center Philosophy
ssc-phil.univie.ac.at/en/organisational-academic-matters/types-of-courses/

University of Vienna
univie.ac.at/en/studies/admission/why-study-here/

University of Vienna
slw.univie.ac.at/en/studying/degree-programmes-with-an-entrance-exam-procedure/#c343354

blog.univie.ac.at/en/how-to-apply-to-the-university-of-vienna-frequently-asked-questions/

slw.univie.ac.at/en/studying/bachelordiploma-programs/

slw.univie.ac.at/studieren/studienbeitrag/hoehe-euewrch-buergerinnen/

slw.univie.ac.at/en/studying/tuition-fee/amount-non-eueeach-citizens/

Vienna University Philharmonic
philharmonie.wien/en

fh campus wien
fh-campuswien.ac.at/fileadmin/redakteure/FH_Campus_Wien/Dokumente/SATZUNG_TeilI_DO_Pruefungsordnung_Anerkennung_16-17_150616_final.pdf

fh-campuswien
fh-campuswien.ac.at/

Vienna University of Technology
tuwien.at/en/studies/international/virtual-welcome-centre/incoming-exchange-students/studies/courses-in-english-language/

Vienna University of Technology
tuwien.at/en/studies/international/virtual-welcome-centre/incoming-exchange-students/studies/german-courses-at-tu-wien/

University of Natural Resources and Life Sciences
boku.ac.at/en/universitaet-fuer-bodenkultur-wien-boku/studieren-an-der-boku/studienangebot/englischsprachige-masterstudien?selectedTypes=group

University of Veterinary Medicine
vetmeduni.ac.at/en/studies/degree-programs/masters-program-comparative-biomedicine/

University of Music and Performing Arts Vienna
mdw.ac.at/398/

University of Applied Arts Vienna
dieangewandte.at/diploma_bachelor_master

Danube University Krems
donau-uni.ac.at/en/studies/course-catalogue.html?queryStr=&submit=1&languages=English

MODULE University Vienna
modul.ac.at/

Webster Vienna Private University
webster.ac.at/

Music and Arts University of the City of Vienna
muk.ac.at/en/programs/study-at-the-muk.html

Music and Arts University of the City of Vienna
muk.ac.at/en/application/german-proficiency.html

Sigmund Freud University
sfu.ac.at/en/academics/

Central European University
ceu.edu/article/2019-03-22/central-european-university-announces-new-vienna-campus

Music Lab University
ammusiclab.com/de

University of Applied Sciences for Management and Communication
fh-vie.ac.at/en/pages/studium/bachelor

University of Applied Sciences for Management and Communication
en.fh-wien.ac.at/home/

Fachhochschule Technikum Wien
technikum-wien.at/studium/bachelor/

Lauder Business School
lbs.ac.at/study-programs/

Distance-Learning University of Applied Sciences
fernfh.ac.at/fernstudium/

IMC University of Applied Sciences Krems
fh-krems.ac.at/studium/

University of Applied Sciences Wiener Neustadt
fhwn.ac.at/en/Studies/Study-Programs

St. Pölten University of Applied Sciences
fhstp.ac.at/de

University of Applied Sciences Burgenland
fh-burgenland.at/en/